The author aged about 21 at Cambridge

First published 2012 by Fast-Print Publishing of Peterborough, England.

www.fast-print.net/store.php

Reading, Writing and Archaeology: An Autobiographical Essay
Copyright © Michael Thompson 2012

ISBN: 978-178035-383-8

A catalogue record for this book is available from the British Library

An environmentally friendly book printed and bound in England
by www.printondemand-worldwide.com

This book is made entirely of chain-of-custody materials

Reading, Writing and Archaeology

An Autobiographical Essay

Michael Thompson

Cambridge 2012

The changes and contradictions seen in us are so flexible that some have imagined that we have two souls, others two angels who bear us company and trouble us each in his own way, one turning us towards good and the other towards evil since such sudden changes cannot be accommodated to one single entity.

Michel de Montaigne, Essays, 11,1,377 (Trs. M.A. Screech)

Preface

The very word "autobiography" immediately suggests vanity and boasting of impressive achievements. Nothing could be further from the intentions of the author in this case. I take a fairly jaundiced view of my life and its shortcomings but hope that with the detachment of old age (I am 83) it may be possible to see past events as near to real as one can hope to achieve and as far as a fairly sombre temprament allows. I try to fit myself into the context of the time and place as seen by an old man and not in the full flood of emotion felt at the time. I am not suggesting my experiences are unique although in one sense they are. We only have one life and so can only know our own experiences and feelings albeit assuming that others have closely similar experiences and feelings. This after all is the basis of poetry or literature. I hope therefore that the reader will perhaps be able to share some of my feelings in a perhaps unusual but in no way extra-ordinary life.

I have never been inclined to keep a diary so in this work I rely almost entirely on memory which in one's eighties is bound to be selective sometimes I fear omitting or distorting important events due to its own limitations. On the other hand there should not be conscious or deliberate omission of matters that one wants to conceal so often encountered in autobiographies.

Obviously matters in my work that particularly concerned me, that is in archaeology and architectural history will deserve more detailed treatment than in other aspects of my life. One has to see the angle from which I perceived events in relation to my age and situation. One is often writing not from direct experience but what has been learned from the media bearing in mind that television plays an increasing part in how we form our views.

The autobiographer always has the problem about the extent to which the first person is employed or 'one' in French style or the third person as with Caesar in the Gallic wars! I hope my solution to this strikes the reader as a suitable resolution.

While I am addressing the general reader most of the time there are parts that may not be readily understood by him if he lacks any knowledge of archaeology and the human figures participating in it. This cannot be helped I fear. Personal experience is the overriding factor and some bias and prejudices will be readily apparent; it may even be that such slants allow the reader to compare his own experiences.

Michael Thompson

Contents

List of Figures

Frontispiece. The author aged about 21 (Ramsey & Muspratt)

1 · The Raj

Normally we have no recollection of the first four years of our lives and the haziness slowly dissipates from then up to the age of six. This was my experience. Certain it is from the birth certificate that I was born in Acton in outer London on 13th August 1928, and equally certain from verbal report that I went with my elder brother, Patrick, by boat on the long three weeks journey via the Suez canal to Bombay (*Mumbai* as it is now). From there we went by train on the 48-hour journey to Calcutta (*Kolkata*). For my 44-year old mother the journey with a baby and a two-year old infant (my brother, Patrick) must have been a very trying experience although she had assistance. Travel by air at that date was virtually unknown. Before we turn to the Raj I may introduce my mother (?1884–1971) and my father (1900–1985).

My mother, Lyla Welman, was born in 1884 (the date is uncertain) to a father described on marriage certificate as a landowner in New South Wales, Australia. Records from Ancestry.co.uk show her ancestry: Harvey Welman, 1782–1869, born in Ireland nr Wexford, the officer Wellman (*Army List*), East Norfolk Regiment who accompanied Wellesley to Portugal in 1808 at the beginning of the Penninsular War and died in Tasmania: John Cameron Welman, 1810–1871 born in England but died in NSW; Arthur Wellesley Welman 1853_1912, born and died in NSW. He was my grandfather having 3 children: Lyla Marie, my mother, Norman 1884–1963, Roy Cameron Patrick,1890–1915 (killed in Galipoli). The use of Wellesley as a Christian name of my grandfather refers to his grandfathers participation in 1808 in Portugal campaign under the Duke of Wellington (before he was Duke).

My mother was a nurse in 1916 in France but when and how she met my father is not certain but probably in India in the early 1920's. My brother was born in India on 16th August 1926. The firm employing my father did not allow marriage for their employees in their youth and her first marriage was in secret, her second secular in England but her conscience caused her to have a Roman Catholic marriage near her death. She was a devout but not active Catholic suggesting an Irish element in her ancestry; my brother and I were brought up Church of England. The marriage certificate shows she deducted some years off her true age while my father added some; he was 16 years younger than her.

About my father, Hartley Thompson, there is much less mystery. He was born in Ipswich February 1900, to a father who was in 'transportation', Pickfords first and later the London North Eastern Railway, moving later to Harlington where my father spent his childhood. My father joined the army in 1918, he did not see service in France but in Ireland and afterwards in India. He left the army in India and joined a Greek firm of jute merchants being first stationed at one of their Bengal plantations our destination in 1928. He assiduously learnt Bengali and Hindi which led to his promotion to position of manager at the Calcutta office. My earliest recollections are from our flat in Calcutta (Kolkata) while he had that job. One of my first memories in a Calcutta kindergarten was biting the arm of a teacher; sudden outbursts of temper have plagued me all my life and cost me dearly. Whether on account of this or to avoid the hot season in the Ganges delta Patrick and I were sent to the south Indian hills? Ooticumund or Bangalore, with suitable escort. I remember little or nothing of the infant school to which we went except some scenes of bad temper, but recall the long 36-hour train journey to Madras (*Chennai*) where we spent a night and I cut myself with a penknife in the bazaar. This was the first of even longer periods of separation from parents, normal for children in the Raj due at least in part to the uncomfortable hot and monsoon seasons and the lack of rapid air transport before independence.

The time in south India was in 1934 as we returned for my father's three yearly leave in February 1935 and I did not return until after the war. Then aged 20 I went on the round-the world Panamerican flight with its frequent stops for refuelling. Bengal had been divided into two by this time with jute plantations in East Pakistan (now Bangledash) so the firm of my father had to seek new trade in the form of imported machinery. The imminent threat of Japanese invasion caused my father to return to part time soldiering and then Independence had shattered the imperial calm of my childhood. The clubs were closing their assets divided among members but little had changed in the way of life in a commercial city like Calcutta. I have been once since to Rajasthan, quite a different part of India,the land of rajahs,where we were caught up in the large military manoeuvres normal behind the Pakistan border.

A child of six years old can hardly have very profound thoughts about his

Fig. 1 ▪ *A stop (? Marseilles) on the voyage home in 1935: Patrick and myself in front with my mother and father holding our topees behind*

Michael Thompson ▪ Cambridge, 2012

environment although if we are to believe Freud it is precisely at this tender age that many of the features of one's later life are laid down. No doubt this was so but far less than by the fairly tempestuous relationship between my father and mother. I will leave this difficult subject and give same general thoughts about India.

For a small European child the poverty, the deformed beggars in the streets come closest to his consciousness and in my case left a deep impression. There were many differences, apart from language, most conspicuous in dress. We wore topees white on Sundays and khaki on weekdays and of course never dhotis. There may have been resemblances between the caste system and the English class system but there was not much else in common, the great void between the two filled only by the unfortunate Anglo-Indians held equally in contempt by both sides. Now I wish I had learnt the languages and developed a closer relationship with the Indians, but then this was all beyond my understanding.

I was ashamed of my father's hostility to Indians right up to his departure for apartheid South Africa in 1955, where he managed a very noisy textile mill up to his retirement. His younger brother, Ernest, stayed on in Calcutta. Most of the people I met in 1948 were lower middle class beguiled by the plethora of servants, the remuneration and the generous leave who felt they had jumped a barrier in the English class system for they certainly could not have achieved such a life style as commuters in London. Who am I to reproach them-my education was largely paid for from there. Women tended to lose out since they really had nothing to do, a stultifying life. Few retired there for they had not put down roots and had relatives in England. My mother being Australian had no inclination to return to England which was one reason why they went to South Africa. My father set to work to learn Afrikaans.

I would not for one moment decry the Raj; English still in general use, the railway network, uniformity of administration and law brought unity to the subcontinent lacking today. Independence was inevitable and desirable but the Raj laid a solid basis on which to build; subsequent events like partition, the terrible massacres of 1947, three wars between India and Pakistan even the recent attack on Mumbai suggest not colonialism but the implacable hatred between Hindu and Muslim is the real problem of the subcontinent. There we must leave the fascinating beginning to my life.

2 · Somerset - Grandparents

On our return from India (we had been back in 1931) we were soon ensconced at Fairmead, the thatched stone cottage at Long Sutton, Somerset, to which my grandfather had retired aged 60 in 1928. This is what I regarded as home from 1935 to 1945 used in school holidays except for a period from 1939 when my grandmother's illness caused us to seek accommodation in several other places. I fear the strain imposed on two old people by having two boys of our age thrust upon them did not occur to my parents nor indeed to ourselves.

Although a 'vernacular' house Fairmead was probably only nineteenth century in age. It had a central through passage, rooms on either side and upstairs two bedrooms in a similar position with a smaller bedroom over the ground-floor passage. Kitchen and outhouse had been added at the back, the latter with a well. Sanitation was provided by an outside earth closet, a small square thatched building over a ditch acting as sewer leading out around the outdoor enclosures. For a small boy going out at night with a torch and open penknife (to repel ghosts) it left a vivid impression. A first floor bathroom had been added on top of the 'cart-house' at the north gable end of the house.

The room on the right as you entered from the street was the 'breakfast room' used continually for all purposes. It had a large table in the middle where all meals were taken and the fireplace was part of a cooking range with oven; cooking was done here or more usually on oil cookers in the kitchen. There was no gas and fuel was coal, coke or peat, rarely wood. The room to the left of the central passage was the drawing room hardly used except on special occasions or private consultation between the doctor and grandfather. The shielded staircase was in here against the west wall.

The extensive property belonging to Fairmead was divided longitudinally by a hedge (except the orchard at the end) and there can be no doubt that two plots had been thrown together to create this large area. Facing the street were two thatched buildings of the same size, Fairmead and the 'barn'.

Michael Thompson ■ Cambridge, 2012

The latter was a shell but the opposed doorways and blocked windows indicate that it had been designed as a house like Fairmead but converted into a 'barn' probably for storing apples. There was space between the two buildings wide enough to contain a gateway leading into the yard behind. A trackway against the right hand side of the property led through two enclosures to the orchard at the end suggesting this belonged to the larger plot with the 'barn' before the two plots were united. There was a large garden behind Fairmead mainly vegetable but soft fruits, plum trees and a small lawn. The apples from the orchard were picked and stored on racks in the barn or in later years knocked down and sent for pressing into cider. (OS 25 in. map Somerset 73/6 confirms separate plots, 388 and 379a).

There was a large barrel for the cider to which my grandfather took a jug at lunchtime to collect drink for the meal. Lunch was the main meal of the day. The apples attracted rats for which phosphorous poison spread on bread was put down with bowls of water to hasten the action of the poison. Traps or gins with spring sides were also employed. One of the most vivid memories of the 'barn' was of my grandfather trying to skewer a rat caught by its hind leg with a fork for a spade is a much better instrument for this purpose. Apart from storage of tools much of the central floor space was filled by a model clockwork railway (Hornby) operated by Patrick.

We must turn our attention now to the occupants of Fairmead. Beyond the dining table Grandpa sat in a Windsor chair on a rubber cushion (he suffered from piles) with his back to the window while Grandma had a rocking chair opposite which she was usually too busy to use. Grandpa controlled the coke bucket which also served as spittoon for he was subject to bouts of coughing. He slept in the Windsor chair in the afternoon. He suffered heart tremors when he indicated the need for brandy. Apart from carving the meat he controlled the parrot, Joey, in the corner of the room and when it was obstreperous went for it with the poker producing deafening shrieks from the bird.

Grandma did the letter writing; they had had seven children all of whom married so there were a lot of letters to write, never less than two or three pages and recorded in a book. Business letters might be dictated to her starting with a sonorous' Gentlemen' from Grandpa. She also read aloud to Patrick and myself which we greatly enjoyed, As she lit the fire in the morning and cooked three times a day (breakfast with a fry-up, substantial lunch and high tea or supper) she was a busy lady. We have omitted washing, darning and knitting (for the troops), bottling and making wine.

Food was rather different from today. Fruit and vegetables came from the garden and I do not recall any being bought. There was no freezer or refrigerator but short-term was done in a square box with grill sides known as a 'safe'. Meat had to be bought except at harvest time when Grandpa shot rabbits bolting from receding cereal, Wine was home made from damsons or blackberries and so on but normally only drunk for royal toasts. The distinctive feature of the diet was the large amount of pastry eaten in the form of pies, fruit and meat, usually one or both each day. Bread and dripping from the weekly joint was an essential part of the diet for Patrick and myself, For the modern dietician the amount of lard fat eaten is horrifying but we both enjoyed it enormously and I certainly make no complaint.

On the passage (hall) side of the breakfast room was the radio in daily use for the News, pretty alarming in wartime, but with some good comedy programmes like Tommy Handley .We did play cards, sevenses, not allowed on Sundays. Grandma read aloud from Kipling, Grahame and so on. I sat on a chair under the window and read a great deal; Dumas, *Gone with the Wind* and so on. At one period we did a lot of photography, developing, printing and even enlarging with a home-made cardboard box contraption; this was all done in the bathroom which we could use as a dark room.

Normally however we were expected to stay outside in the garden or barn. We took long walks to the neighbouring small towns of Somerton, Langport or Martock, much more accessible once we had bicycles from 1940. For major shopping Yeovil was the choice but the ultimate was Taunton.

Patriotism was more like that of the first world war: if the national anthem was played we all stood to attention. The constant reverses to our forces in the early years of the war were difficult to stomach but if any excesses of the Germans were mentioned on the radio Grandma would cry out in horror 'cowards' or 'devils'. Their prize set of aluminium cooking pans were taken out in the yard and holed with a pick so the metal could go for aircraft manufacture. I am glad that neither of my grandparents lived to see the Empire dissolved; it would have been too painful.

Religion was important: there was a huge family bible with photographs and records going back two previous generations. Certain things were forbidden on Sundays like playing cards, laundry, festivities of any kind and so on. The church service on the radio was always listened to by Grandma at least. She occasionally attended matins at the village church with me sometimes; Patrick and Grandpa were quite indifferent to religion but at this time I said a trilogy of prayers in bed (if I did not fall asleep), a creed, a prayer of my own composition and the Lord's prayer.

What emerges clearly from the Fairmead experience is the Victorian elements in my make-up derived from there. I became very much the passive younger brother following the lead that Patrick gave, and to some extent it has been that pattern of behaviour that I followed in later life but with someone else standing in for Patrick. There was an interruption for a year or two after Grandma's illness in 1939 but the alternative places we stayed for the holidays I will deal with later. Grandparents are not really a substitute for physical parents but I was lucky and would regard this as a very happy period of my life.

3 · Devonshire - Boarding School

My time at Allhallows School Honiton (Rousdon, near Lyme Regis from 1938 closed down about 2002),1935-45 ran parallel to holidays at Fairmead. My parents left Patrick and me there in May 1935, we saw them in 1938 but then owing to the war not again until the summer of 1945 after the end of the European war. No leave was possible in 1941. It was quite normal for parents from the UK domiciled in India to leave their children in boarding school in England, perhaps giving them a better education than they would have had otherwise. What was unusual in our case was the long period of separation from parents and inflicting us on elderly grandparents for ten years.

The school at Honiton did not occupy a single building but was scattered with the core of chapel and dining hall near the town church with the head-master's house holding the junior school to which I belonged on the opposite side of the high street. Bear in mind that I was six and a half years old when I started. The usual washing facilities of earthenware ewer and basin for each occupant in a small dormitory prevailed with the water some-times freezing in the unheated room. A young Scottish matron and teacher (at whose home I spent Christmas holiday 1939) became close friends which made for a very pleasant life.

Other memories of Honiton are less pleasant. Walking down the High street to the housemaster's lodgings to be beaten was a shock. Chastisement was normal at that time and for much longer but my father using a slipper was a very different experience from the shock of four or six sharp blows on the backside in a bent-over position. Once I saw the flogging in front of the school of boys by the headmaster for smoking at a later date, the most dramatic case I know of.

Another memory sticking in my mind is of the lurid silent German films industrial and futuristic shown in the evenings. There were of course silent American films of Charlie Chaplin and Buster Keaton. The food provided by the school was I think sparse and supplemented by items that we brought to

Michael Thompson ▪ Cambridge, 2012

the school in tuckboxes which we all had. Bulk was provided by spreading sauces on bread or even pepper and salt and mustard. We must have been hungry! I fear I have very little recollection of the actual teaching. We saw ourselves as very different from the local boys, the 'brickies' as we called them with whom there was same degree of hostility.

It was a profound change from an urban to a rural setting when the school moved from Honiton to Rousdon, near Lyme Regis (postal address Dorset) in the summer of 1938: instead of a scatter of buildings the school; was concentrated in a large 19th century mansion with its attached estate of two or three hundred acres. The economic circumstances of the time allowed it to be purchased at a modest price. We must pause to describe the setting designed as a wealthy man's seat not a school.

Entering from the main road by the North Lodge gateway the drive swung right through woodland concealing the school. A track on the · left· led to the burnt-out remains of a nineteenth century observatory some of whose recordings of rainfall, temperature and air pressure survive. Emerging from the wood the house is in front with large grass areas on either side of the drive converted into playing fields by the school. A striking feature of these fields were large cylindrical pillars about two metres high curved at the top which although resembling phallic symbols were more mundanely scratching pillars for cows when the area was pasture. Before the forecourt of the buildings was a crossroads the road on the right leading to the West Lodge and on the left to the East Lodge, both inhabited by masters. The road on the right passed the church, same date as the house about which Pevsner was so damning (the architect, George, was not a favourite) and further on the home farm again of the same date. Passing into a courtyard on the left a gate led to the bowling green, a long level area of green grass, perhaps actually intended for bowls; on the right a gateway led to a bridge over a ramp to take vehicles down to the cellars and beyond this an arched entry beneath a clock tower that led to stables and coach houses converted by the school into laboratories.

The house itself is described by Pevsner perhaps rather harshly as of 'a rather grim Franco-Flemish sixteenth century style' but was perhaps attempting a vaguely medieval or Tudor style. One passed through a *porte cochère* with a room above occupied by a master. On entering there was a large hall on the left open to the roof and with a large fireplace. At the 'upper' end of the hall a doorway led to the square tower that rose above the hall. A master lived in this but only known to me as the place where we did our 'firewatching' during the war. The hall was used by the school for assemblies, morning prayers, performances, even for boxing in a ring constructed in the middle. The hall had a gallery at the lower end with an organ in it. There was no kitchen beyond the screens end of the hall but on the other side of the passage there was a pleasant room serving perhaps originally as an office which became a classroom.

The corridor with mosaic floor led south past a grand marble stair case on the right to a set of grand rooms on ground and first floor that enjoyed fine views over the sea; evidently where the family actually lived. The school had its dining room here possibly reusing the original while the kitchen again probably in its former position lay at extreme west of the building in what must have been servants' quarters. There were two courtyards divided by a central range which terminated in the entry. There was cellarage under most of the building which was used in one case as a 22 rifle range but principally beneath the hall converted into a chapel for Sunday services, confirmation and so on. Pevsner never entered the building which may not be of great beauty but has a fascinating design and on my impression lent itself very well to adaptation as a boarding school for 150 or so boys. The architects were Vaughan and George, the latter being Sir Ernest George (1839-1922) noted for introducing French and Flemish features of the sixteenth century into his buildings. The Peake family for whom all this was built left two unforgettable features behind them: a fine said to be almost complete collection of stuffed birds on the first floor and two huge full size portraits of the Peakes who built the mansion hung at the upper end of the hall.

In 1938 I had an unusual experience; I was quite ill with measles following an injection and chicken pox confined to a south-facing room on the south front overlooking the sea. I saw a coast with fields and houses on the horizon, clearly not France which was too far away but presumably a sort of reflexive mirage, not really explained then or since. Beyond the terrace on the south front was a field used for tennis courts and beyond this a ha-ha separated it from pasture. Beyond this wooded broken ground from landslips passed down to the beach and sea.

Turning now to activities within the school the daily routine started at 7.15 and after breakfast assembly in the great hall for morning prayer and announcements. The morning was filled by lessons of three quarters of an hour each requiring movement with books between classrooms and laboratories. After lunch came compulsory games: rugby in the winter term, hockey in the Easter term and cricket in the summer term. There were two further lessons after games. After supper or high tea there was 'prep' private study at a desk in the common room of each 'house' ,and finally bed. Sunday was quite different, no lessons but we wore suits and there were two chapel services of about an hour beneath the hall. A memorable feature was baths, once a week or after games as required. We had eight baths in the basement with three boys in each their feet hanging over the side. It was a noisy, steamy affair, punctuated by screams when the hot water was let into the bath. It was all very enjoyable but not for the faint-hearted. Much of the classroom heating was by antracite stoves which were very effective. One day a week there were 'scouts' for the younger boys or OTC, Officer Training Corps, which as a concession to social change altered its title to JTC, Junior Training Corps, in the course of the war. For a year or two we still wore puttees ,jackets with brass buttons and peaked hats as if it was the 1914-18 war we fought, but battle dress was introduced in I think 1942. We no longer polished buttons but spent time on the boots. The Corps paraded in the car park in front of the school under the command of a teacher/officer, and there was a week's camp under canvas each summer. As a solitary boy, I was not very fond of uniforms although. I have to admit that I learnt some useful things: shooting with small calibre rifles, the 24-hour clock, maps and map references, judging ranges and so on.

As compulsory games have been discussed often I will only briefly mention them here. It is a question of temperament but for the solitary without a very combative spirit disliking the dressing up beforehand there was no pleasure in them. Running was suited to my temperament and I even tried my hand at boxing feeling something of a martyr for the house.

In the senior school classes were graded a,b,c according to ability. The aim of the teaching was to raise the level of the pupil to the point that at 16 he could obtain a pass, credit or even distinction in the School Certificate (cf. GCSB today) or Higher Certificate (Cf. A level) at 18. I took the School Certificate at 13 and Higher Certificate at 15. Although I regarded myself as a humanist I took Chemistry and Geography as subsidiary subjects in Higher Certificate which has been useful since. Patrick was an outstanding mathematician so we had little in common.

Although some west country cities like Plymouth, Exeter and Bristol suffered severely in the 'Blitz' I personally never heard a bomb or V1 or V2 explode but this does not mean we were unaffected by the war which would have been impossible, We heard of the terrible defeats in the early part of the war, we listened to Churchill's speeches in 1940; we invited soldiers who had escaped at Dunkirk to tea; there was rationing of increasing severity and the black-out was applied to every door and window and car head-lights. In the latter part of the war we had to spend two-hour shifts in the tower fire-watching, principally to man the telephone to call for assitance in the event of enemy attack. The most poignant effects of the war were the names posted up of old boys often only 19-20 years old killed in action, sometimes known personally to myself. They were from all arms of the services but especially RAF bomber command, air crew and rear gunners. Although there were antinvasion measures (mining of land adjoining the sea and the huge hole dug in the road to the beach known as the 'tank-trap') there was never the loss of confidence and resignation to defeat found in the eastern counties, except perhaps in a master of South African origin. The visitor to the school would hardly have known there was a war on. I hardly saw an American soldier except at the Collinson's in Exeter and the memorable walk I did on VE day 1945 from the school to Fairmead (30 miles).

Mention must be made of holidays from 1939 when we were not able to go to Fairmead: with remote relatives of my mother at Middleton-on-sea in the summer of 1939, with a City friend of my father in the same year, with the schoolteacher I mentioned at Malvern Christmas 1939. In 1940 Patrick and I spent the summer holiday at school in that vast building which was an experience, especially as I learnt to ride and acquired a bicycle with one or two tumbles. At what point we started to use the Collinsons on the outskirts of Exeter I am not sure. It was an extraordinary house without electricity so we used oil lamps and candles and slept in an old railway carriage. The Collinsons kept a cow so milk and clotted cream were always available. Here I first encountered a girl, almost an alien specie for us, but I was not seriously stirred until later in Spain.

I left Allhallows School at the end of the summer term,1945, when my parents were on leave from India, the European war having ended but not the Japanese war, the two atomic bombs were dropped during their stay in this country. I lived in London where my father arranged for me to go to a crammer in Holland Park while living at a Toc H hostel in Notting Hill Gate where I stayed off and on for the next two or three years.

At the crammer I was supervised by a fairly left-wing teacher which brought me in touch with a wide range of unfamiliar matters, for Atlee had replaced Churchill and a new world was being created. The Toc H hostel was a short distance from the underground and not far from Kensington Gardens. I could take long walks through the West End in the early hours when it was virtually empty except of course for the ubiquitous prostitutes who could be quite aggressive. At the hostel I met a young pianist whose intensive practice reverberated throughout the building (formerly the Greek embassy) with whom I became quite friendly. In a long walk he explained to me that he was gay (the word was not used in that sense then) which had caused trouble with his father. Homosexuality was at that time an offence punishable by imprisonment. I was interested but felt no repugnance for sexual matters were something that bored me. At school I did not or could not masturbate and felt a little different from the other boys. I tackled my father as to whether the circumcision I had had done in India for medical reasons had rendered me impotent but he dismissed the idea entirely. So the matter went no further.

The climax of my studies in Holland Park which consisted of fairly general essays was the entry exam to Pembroke College. Cambridge, held at the college in December 1945. After it I had gone down to Long Sutton to spend Christmas with my grandparents the last visit as it turned out (my grandfather died in February 1946 and my grandmother in June); as the TocH hostel did not know the address they did not forward the telegram from London which I found on my return telling me that I had been awarded an exhibition and was expected at the College in a fortnight. A letter from the Chief Tutor told me that the historical papers I did were not of a very high standard but I had done a very good essay. Imagination was my strong point then and since. An exhibition is the third sort of award after major and minor scholarships. To the surprise of my parents and the school (who had never had an Oxbridge award) I was in the University. The six months after leaving school in Devon were well spent: I began to familiarize myself with the capital, town against rural life. London was very run down, bombed in the City and East End while the west was very dilapidated. The peeling paintwork of Victorian terraces in Bayswater or Paddington sticks in my mind. The West End was a lively place; I had been starved of cinema and theatre in Devon and Somerset but I now saturated myself. I was not in lodgings but in pleasant company in the Toe H hostel, albeit with some of the piety of the first world war still prevailing.

I shall conclude this chapter at this point and turn to my life as a conscript 1946-48,for although I was at Cambridge Easter and summer terms 1946 I went into the army in the autumn returning to Cambridge in October 1948 and remaining there until 1953. It seemed wiser to treat the Cambridge experience as a whole in the next chapter but one.

4 . The Army

I was 18 in August 1946 and so was called up in the normal way in I think November although I forget the name of the first barracks (Oxford) where I started, although I have a vivid recollection of the first six weeks in a wooden hut. I suppose there were thirty of us, all from the East End of London except myself and one from Brighton promptly called 'Brighton' by everyone else. In England the classes tend to be kept rigidly apart but in the barrack room they are mixed up. My companions were all very friendly except Brighton. The Cockney humour with which I was deluged was an experience to be savoured and not forgotten. It was one of the most enjoyable periods of six weeks that I had in the army.

At this date in 1946 the Japanese war had finished and the Korean war not yet started so the main objective was to disperse and send home the huge body of men still under arms. They did not need officers but wished rather to dispense with as many as possible. A solution to the problem of conscripts regarded as officer material was to put them into limbo with the title of 'Other Ranks 1'. It was with this improbable title of OR1 that I was sent to Northern Ireland, to Palace Barracks, Hollywood just East of Belfast.

I found myself with 20 or so other ORI's not in the barracks but in an abandoned adjoining camp of Nissen huts formerly holding prisoners of war. There had been a lack of maintenance so we tended to move from one hut to another as the roof leaks made the former hut untenable. This was December with the sole form of heating a stove fuelled only with wood which meant time had to be spent foraging for wood. The fumes were appreciable and as we tried to seal all apertures it is a wonder we were not asphyxiated. This was the winter of 1946–7 of exceptional severity when the coal trains were not able to reach London bringing the country almost to a halt. The sanitation was in unroofed enclosures so one has vivid recollections of clearing seats of snow and frost when using them.

Things became easier in the spring; oddly enough I look back on this period in Ireland as one of the happiest I had in the army. There was no conscription nor rationing in the province and I was astonished to be able to, buy a pint of milk in the street from the milkman for milk was rationed like much else in England. The 'troubles' were some 23 years ahead but there was still constant security from the earlier 'troubles'. Rifles had to be locked together without bolts. The mobile patrol usually ended up peeling potatoes since they were not called out while I was there. On sentry duty we had five live rounds which were kept in the pocket, not loaded in the rifle. The people were friendly and only once did I meet with hostility. Wearing civilian clothes you could travel everywhere including the Republic; I went as far as Dublin.

I had not learnt about the economy of the truth and on the whole platoon being asked if anyone disliked the army I was the only one who said that I did not; it probably cost me a commission for I did not get through a selection board! Looking back I doubt if I was cut out for the role of officer in the infantry, so although at the time it was disappointing it was probably to my advantage.

When I left Ireland in 1947 for Colchester barracks, Essex; it was presumably there that I was made up to Sergeant in the RAEC (Royal Army Education Corps) This required three months training before actually teaching, one month's drill course at the Guards depot at Pirbright and two months practice teaching at a place in Exhibition Road. The former was of particular interest.

We were about twenty in a hut with a guardsman' trained soldier' in charge of 30 sergeants whose mess we used, but it is perhaps indicative of the disdainful attitude that we did not have an NCO in charge. Guards officers who are a rather special breed of men, or were then, blamed teachers, RAEC in particular, for influencing the voters that had caused the calamity of the social upheaval of a Labour government. I still have fine :memories of muster parades when from a position well to the back we watched the adjutant come out on horseback, and the frightening inspection of the guardsmen (not us !).

Of the teacher training I have little recollection although it dawned on me that teaching was not my forte. Memories are a little overshadowed by recalling the uncouth pre-war warrant officer whom we had the misfortune to encounter, Preliminaries completed I was assigned to the Royal Millitary School of Music at Richmond not to teach music but to teach bandboys. There were three categories at the school: a small number learning to conduct a band, those learning to play an instrument and the bandboys who had enlisted if I remember rightly at age 14. They were completing their education and if I recall rightly I taught map-reading and possibly mathematics. As I still lived at the Toc H hostel I made a very long bus journey morning and evening to and from the School. Concerts were given at week-ends where one helped but otherwise it was a Monday to Friday job.

I was still a considerable reader in most of my spare time particularly on the bus journeys from the School and on one of these I had my road to Damascus by reading Gordon Childe's *What happened in history* in a Penguin edition. Childe was an Australian, a classicist at Oxford but turned his attention to archaeology publishing scholarly works in the 1920's. 1930's. 1940's on British, European and Near Eastern fields. The most famous was of course *The Dawn of European Civilisation*, 1925, which ran to five editions and was our textbook at Cambridge. He worked out a scheme, essentially a diffusionist one of the development of agriculture and urbanisation spreading from the Near East through Europe. It made a coherent story relating the finds in different areas and although much modified since is still the foundation of our thinking. Suddenly I saw the subject not as a form of antiquarianism but as something with real meaning justifying scholarly study which profoundly influenced me later at Cambridge.

I was also influenced by Childe's tragic death in 1957 when he committed suicide by falling from a cliff in his homeland area in Australia. He had no wife or children, no close relatives or friends on his retirement, his powers were perhaps weakening (he was possibly overfond of whisky). Moreover his deeply committed communist views must have had a bad shock: by the Soviet suppression of the Hungarian rising of 1956 which so disillusioned Continental communists. In addition the first rumblings of radiocarbon dating would hardly be compatible with his interpretations of Europe's past. It was clear that one cannot live by archaeology alone and political beliefs need to be flexible.

I left the army in the summer of 1948 returning to Cambridge in October; to that we must turn in the next chapter. The army experience had left me wiser; some parts of it may have even given me pleasure and enjoyment.

5 · Cambridge

As explained I came up to Pembroke College. Cambridge in January 1946, having obtained an history exhibition the previous month but after the Easter and summer terms I was called up only returning to college in October 1948.

The College is a forbidding place in December when. I took the entry exam and January, 1946, when 1 came up with rationing at its worst including bread and solid fuel which provided most of the heating. I was in college in a fine room with six windows on three sides overlooking the garden, beautiful in summer or spring but decidedly exposed and cold in winter. The coal ration only allowed heating on four days so one had to go to a cinema on the other three days to keep warm. I had a gas jet but no gas fire attached. Now it houses the Chief Tutor with my little bedroom housing his secretary, all properly heated. In my time there was no sanitation only ewer and basin and chamber pot; for bath and toilet one had to cross the adjoining court. Being on the first floor over the junior parlour there tended to be a thunderous noise from men in their mid-twenties returned from the war and full of joy. I was only 17 years old but smoked quite heavily like most people at the time, especially a pipe; I was overawed but not unhappy.

I was reading history, the subject of the exhibition and had the normal essays and lectures. Particularly agreeable were the reading parties arranged by the Dean when one went by train to a remote hotel, reading in the morning and taking long walks in the afternoon. I fear bridge groups often developed occupying time on the journeys and destination, not at all the intended purpose.

There were no women in the college apart from bedmakers in the morning although there were two colleges for women not fully recognised as members of the University. Gowns had to be worn at hall, lectures, after dark and on all formal occasions such as seeing an officer of the college. The colleges were locked at night and more or less impenetrable after midnight without clambering over walls. I need not pursue these well known matters merely saying that the conspicuous changes today are the pervasive female presence, disappearance of gowns and the improvements in heating and sanitation.

When I returned to Pembroke in October 1948 two important changes took place in my circumstances : the first of these I was paid a government grant for further education and training, making me much less dependent on subsidy from my father (the exhibition only yielded a nominal sum). There was no question of full support or loans. More important I was no longer in college but in 'digs', lodgings licensed by the University, in effect bed and breakfast with a room of variable size in anything from a widow's lounge to a first floor bedroom in a family house. The rent had been set by the University although there might be an extra charge far fuel. I never returned to a room in college up to leaving in 1953.

My first lodgings were near the station in a first-floor bedroom where drinking parties upset the landlady and where I myself was unhappy. I had some doubts about my sanity so sought medical advice and took a course of psychoanalysis in Grantchester. Real improvement only came when I moved to a ground-floor room on the other side of Cambridge and also left the rather bleak and impersonal history faculty for the small and friendlier archaeology and anthropology faculty. It will be remembered that I had been convinced of the intellectual basis for archaeology reading Childe; It was a change that was to influence the course of the rest of my life. I shared lodgings with a Dutch researcher at the Low Temperature research laboratory who provided congenial friendship. I knew a few friends from the army but I was rather isolated, being averse to joining various sports such as rowing.

In 1949 I had my BA degree for under wartime regulations that could be awarded after five terms which I had of course done. I did not know then that I would stay on for part two of the archaeology trips or even less that I would spend three years further doing a PhD. Thoughts turned to a career and I consulted a rather weary and unenthusiastic adviser at the career centre for advice, there are he said three alternatives: teaching, the colonial service or industry. My army experience of teaching had not been encouraging and I found industry daunting. There were six-month courses in customs and languages of particular areas which were very popular. I did think about it but now we know that the colonial service disappeared 15-20 years later I have no regrets about not taking that worthwhile road. The obloquy that attaches to colonies and 'colonialism' now was unknown then except perhaps in the Soviet Union and colonial administrators were held in some esteem.

I lived by this time a fairly satisfying life heavily fantasizing not about women as yet but patriotism or retaliation for insults or indeed any pleasant thing. I travelled everywhere by bicycle from ' digs' to lectures or supervisions or out in the evening. I was free of college restrictions but still had to wear a gown after dark, on one occasion had to pay a fine of 13/4d when caught without a gown after dark. 13s 4d if you had your BA or 6s 8d if you were still an undergraduate.

It is time to turn to actual studies: following my return to Cambridge I kept up history for a year; I remember little of the lecturers except someone who lectured on historiography in the seventeenth century, not a tripos subject but he had a loyal audience. At my change to archaeology Grahame Clark (not yet succeeding Dorothy Garrod as Professor, whose lectures I attended) had just started the excavation of the well known mesolithic site of Star Carr near Scarborough. I think I went in 1949 when we were all accommodated in an old railway carriage. The waterlogged site which had to be pumped out each day provided splendid preservation of bone, antler and of course wood; what better introduction to the subject could there have been. Apart from Professor Garrod Glyn Daniel the expert on megaliths lectured on the history of archaeology. He later made his name on television as chairman of 'Animal, Vegetable, Mineral" which so popularised archaeology with the general public. Although the later neolithic and bronze age in the Mediterranean were most popular because of their ancestry to the Classical world I preferred and chose the early period with unforeseen consequences described below.

The main outlook at Cambridge so far as archaeology is concerned was and is palaeolithic and mesolithic and to a lesser degree neolithic and bronze age, the Roman period and middle ages were regarded as matters for Classicists and historians. The elevation of the Prehistoric Society to a national society in 1935 emphasised this. In this respect it caused a separation from outside where the main interest is in the literate periods with a more insular attitude towards the subject. There is quite a gulf which sadly can lead to hostility; no one has suffered more from this rancour than the present writer when he ventured into the world outside Cambridge; baleful eyes across the interview table have only too often reminded him of this.

Prehistory is a child of evolution which opened almost limitless passages of time from when man first appeared as a distinct creature to the recent present when man made himself to quote Childe and the various literate societies developed. Childe in spite of his Oxford background was a dyed-in-the wool prehistorian looking from the back forwards while the historian like the archaeologist of later periods tends to look from the front backwards; the student of Rome can lose himself in nostalgic admiration. It may be useful at this point to look at the other giant in archaeology in the middle years of the last century which reveals the deep division of outlook that prevails equally today.

Childe we have met already with his massive knowledge and scholarship and disengagement from the practicalities of fieldwork and excavation, theory-led as it were. For Sir Mortimer Wheeler for whom discipline and neatness in excavation was the great principle in archaeology there could hardly be a greater contrast but this must not let us deny his considerable achievements in discoveries in this country and India. Perhaps even greater was his work as Secretary of the British Academy galvanising that fairly recumbent body into founding overseas schools and his spreading of the good news to the general public on television as a sort of iconic figure. Nothing suited him better than to share the glory of the people that he was studying, notably the Roman Empire and he belonged one feels to our own Imperial past notably as Director of Antiquities in the dying days of the Raj; there could hardly be greater contrast with Childe. We need both kinds of men.

We may end this chapter on a happy note: a scheme had been started that involved taking the students just before the exams in the summer term (my final exam was in 1950) for two or three days to an important pre-historic site staying in a local inn or hotel. In my case it was in the inn within the earthwork at Avebury, Wiltshire from where Silbury Hill, the avenues and so on could be visited. I think we took the coach to Stonehenge which is some miles to the south. The whole trip is firmly implanted in my mind as one of my happiest experiences, as much from the companionship as from the monuments.

The change from undergraduate to research student meant a different way of life: no lectures or supervision, hardly eating in college and thrown more on one's own resources. The period of research for the PhD I will deal with in the next chapter.

Michael Thompson ▪ Cambridge, 2012

6 ▪ Spain

What I had intended to do when I finished part 2 of the tripos I can no longer remember, I had been to eastern Spain under my own steam to see some of those wonderful rock paintings of leaping and hunting figures. This was Franco's Spain only twelve years after the civil war with high security, police checking papers in the trains and everywhere. I had to warn the regional police that I was going into the mountains in caseI was mistaken for a brigand or political opponent. Cars were a privilege and I slightly damaged my taxi on rocks looking for a painting. The trip taken alone was not as successful as I had hoped. However my interest was known to the Professor now Grahame Clark who had succeeded Dorothy Garrod following her unexpected early retirement.

Clark it will be remembered had started his excavation at the waterlogged site of Star Carr in 1949. He was anxious to know how the methods of working the profusion of red deer antler at his site compared with the upper paleolithic worked antler in France and north Spain. At the time the Catalan professor of archaeology at Barcelona, Luis Pericot, an English speaker and frequent visitor to England made such a visit; Clark arranged that I should study at Barcelona under Pericot which I did for six months or so in 1951. Pericot had a distinguished record as the excavator of Parpalló, the well known cave with extensive upper paleolithic remains in eastern Spain, and the author of a book on Catalan megaliths.

For Franco's Spain one needed a visa; one went by train from Paris and changed trains at the border. My first *pensione* was simply taken by choosing one of the numerous touts at the station but Pericot found me a lodge with three old ladies (nick named *las viejitas*) in a flat or *piso* in central Barcelona. I had my breakfast (not an English one!) there and ate out in town. I was deeply impressed by the grid plan of Barcelona, its sunken railways, the Gaudi buildings and so on. Nowadays the city is too well known for me to say more.

I spent most of the time studying in the museum where I had one of the great experiences of my life, meeting a Catalan girl whose name may be omitted. I fell passionately in love, quite intoxicated. I had no idea that this sort of thing happened in real life. Her father was a well-known doctor and she lived in a flat (*piso*) in the Gaudi building in the *Ramblas*. We met there and also at Oxford where she studied Greek pottery prompted by the large amount of material from *Ampurias* on the Catalan coast. She later married a colleague from the museum at Barcelona. Much of my later life has been haunted by doubts about whether I should have resolutely pushed matters further to a happy conclusion. A non-earning student, lacking self-confidence was not in a strong position and I now much doubt whether very different temperaments could have made a lasting union.

I must return to my studies in the perninsula. Pericot furnished me with introductory cards suitably annotated in Castilian or Catalan according to the first language of the recipient. I moved southwards to visit Tarragona, Castellon, Valencia. Castellon was the centre for east Spanish rock art unfortunately not associated with an industry leaving the dating to be a matter of lively controversy. Pericot had himself excavated a mesolithic rock shelter known as *la Cocina* (the Kitchen) I drew microliths from there in the *Diputación* at Valencia if I recall rightly. At that time I had little to detain me in the east or south (bearing in mind that the title of my thesis was 'Some mesolithic cultures of the Iberian peninsula), so I had little contact to my regret with Moorish Spain.

Madrid had plenty of material from the north in the museum and I think I went there twice. On one occasion I was driven by an Aragonese archaeologist, who was of sufficiently high status to have the use of a car with a chauffeur, to the city through January snow. In this case I encountered the arrogant and hostile attitude of the non-Catalan Spaniard for I was lucky to be in Catalonia where the attitude towards foreigners was much more friendly. A colleague of mine who went to Madrid had to beat a retreat because of the attitude of the professor at the University. The victorious Franco regime ruled and Catalan was forbidden in publication. Pericot was an unusual figure in the learned world in Spain.

I also visited several museums in north Spain, particularly Santander, as far west as Oviedo. There had been large-scale cave excavations there in the beginning of the last century. The particular interest here was that the antler used for tool-making was that from red deer and not reindeer as in France. I remember particularly writing to my girl friend in Barcelona comparing the stormy seas of the Bay of Biscay to the milder waves of the Mediterranean indicating the strength of the passions in my area!

The title of the thesis referred to the whole Iberian peninsula so there still remained Portugal where the shell middens (heaps of kitchen waste, mainly shells) upstream from Lisbon on the Tagus at Mugem were well known from the nineteenth century. I drew any of the flint mircoliths that were available and plotted the sites of the seven or eight known middens. I was extremely lucky in that Dorman Long who had been building a new bridge over the Tagus provided the section of the river bed with their borings made beforehand. This showed an enormous depth of gravel the underlying rock only reached at one point. A most ingenious method of overcoming this problem was to bind the piles at the top so they spread out below resisting subsidence. The supports for the bridge rested above this on a platform on top of the gathered piles.

The depth of deposited gravel near Lisbon provided evidence of prolonged recent filling of the valley while 16th and 17th century maps indicated that even then the salt-water estuary extended further up than it does today. No doubt a rising sea level caused it to silt up. The shells in the middens showed the midden-makers were eating estuarine clams. I regret that this interesting piece of work did not achieve full publication.

A most enjoyable experience which led to some thoughts on Portugal was a memorable picnic held close to one of the Mugem midddens. A colleague from Cambridge sadly no longer with us, and myself were invited to stop at his country residence by the Marques de Cardaval and while there to a picnic at Mugem near a midden. We drove there when two lorries arrived one with tables and chairs for the picnic and the other holding food and drink in ample quantities together with a veritable alcoholic bar. There were of course waiters to serve us; there was a feeling of the *anicen regime* about the whole event. Portugal had escaped the socialist government and civil war of neighbouring Spain so rural society had changed much less since the nineteenth century. It was a revealing experience, albeit enjoyable, about Salazar's Portugal although we must not forget to thank our kind host.

The method of working the antler at Star Carr had particularly aroused the interest of Professor Clark and whether it derived from the earlier reindeer antler working in France. So I made a special journey to south west France and Paris with a large borrowed plate camera to photograph what antler remains were in France throwing light on the problem. The method was to set camera with tripod on the floor focusing with a cigarette packet or match box (I smoked 20 cigarettes a day at that time), replacing this with a piece of worked antler and allowing a long exposure in the poor light of most museums with open aperture. It was a primitive but effective way of doing the job. Many of the prints of these plates are used in the second volume of my thesis. The main problem was of course the weight of the plates and equipment to carry around.

The fragments of antler were small so the technique of working was not always clear although the stumps left behind suggest the whole beam was employed; we have to remember that only bits thought to be worth keeping found their way to the museum, presumably as samples of a lot of waste. It was almost exclusively reindeer antler which has a twisted beam and much less soft core so the usable outer bone (antlers are regrown annually) is much thicker than in red deer antler. On the other hand the outer bone is smoother, brittle, denser and less elastic than with red deer, so it might be easier to work with the sawing, planing movement found to be the secret of working red deer antler. They both had a lot in common and the reindeer antler may indeed have been more yielding with a sharp flint.

My own experiments on Scottish red deer antler demonstrated to my satisfaction that prolonged soaking prior to work was essential, that the grooves were made by paring or planing with a suitably sharp flake and that a strip could be readily extracted by slipping a thong underneath sliding along to free the strip which could then be snapped out. I made an Azilian head from a strip and using experiments with pillows concluded these curious heads were intended to toggle beneath the animal's skin. This was made necessary to resist the dangling shaft catching in the incoming vegetation. I fear this controversial view may be difficult for the general reader. The material from experiments has been deposited at the British Museum together with a copy of the thesis.

The typing and binding of the thesis was completed in 1953 and approved

Michael Thompson ■ Cambridge, 2012

by the two examiners in the same year thus being completed in the minimum three years allowed for such a dissertation, a speed unusual in archaeology. I regret not having made more use of it, but I had to make a living as we shall see below.

Apart from my time in Spain, Portugal and France I lived in Cambridge and only when I joined the Ministry of Works in 1954 did I move to London and take up quarters, bed and breakfast, in Ebury Street from where the story is continued below.

7 · Russian Translation

I had found that for certain matters in connection with antler working there were valuable ethnographic parallels in Siberia and that a reading knowledge of Russian was useful. I vividly recall learning Russian vocabulary on the train from Paris to Barcelona. In any case with the 'cold war' then at its height there were other matters in the Soviet Union that interested me. Childe's extreme views aroused my curiosity for as we have seen he had opened my eyes to archaeology as a viable subject intellectually. The Soviet Union did not subscribe to international copyright conventions and translations took place freely without permission. My initiation into Russian translation was however quite unexpected.

The founder of Penguins, Sir Allen Lane, had been travelling in China and the Soviet Union; he wanted a book on Russian archaeology. The Soviet archaeologists had been suffering something of a tirade from Russian emigres in the USA. They did not want emigre archaeology unfortunately as there was a good emigre Polish archaeologist in this country at that time. Unlike today at that time it was virtually impossible to get to Russia except with a trade union or if you were very distinguished. My advice was sought and I replied that there was really no choice except to translate the book by Mongait, even if it was violently political. To my astonishment Penguin asked whether I would do the translation. As I had no knowledge of the spoken language and had never set foot in Russia I hesitated before I agreed to do so.

I think it took three or four years before my translation (slightly adapted) appeared under the title *Archaeology in the USSR*. Meanwhile when we were in press the Russians had produced a hardback English translation of their own done by a Czech student with I fear many shortcomings. I learnt very quickly the golden rule that you always translate into your native language; to translate from one foreign language into another produces an ugly text with egregious errors. I was given the copyright and received a royalty for the Penguin translation. I felt it slightly necessary to adapt the text by reducing numbers of 'bourgeois archaeologists' applied to the west and one or two political diatribes. Reviews were favourable and sales ran into many thousands. There was even a second edition; a friend picked up a copy in the market at Cambridge fifty years after publication.

The Soviet Union covered a much larger area than the Russian Federation of today so that the book provided information on many remote areas. I have seen it quoted in footnotes quite recently. Mongait was to some extent responding to bitter attacks from emigre archaeologists in the USA, but discounting this it was a fruitful period in Russian archaeology in the 1950's and 1960's so it was a suitable time for the translation. Funds seem to have been available for excavation and publication that are not available today. There was at that time a better larger book on the same subject produced by the Academy of Sciences, although less suitable for the general reader.

As we have seen Gordon Childe killed himself in 1957 possibly caused to some extent by the Soviet suppression of the Hungarian rising in 1956. Childe had been *persona grata* in the Soviet Union because of his scholarship and communist views but in archaeology there was an important difference of view. Childe was a classicist by origin so it is not a surprise that his thinking depended on diffusion from the east Mediterranean as a governing factor: it is the *Leitmotiv* of his books. Soviet archaeologists were firm supporters of autocthonous development, and did not wish people to feel they were descended from recent arrivals. It is the old debate about diffusion in slightly different dress. The recent reaction to the 'invasion theory' in this country has clear affinity with the old Soviet view. The truth no doubt lies somewhere between the two extremes but fascinating as the subject is we can hardly pursue it here. As almost the entire population of the USA is descended from those who came by boat we can hardly disbelieve in invasion altogether!

The publication of the translation from Mongait aroused much interest in Russian archaeology and my next translation was not of my choice although the subject interested me because of my experiments with working antler. It is one of the perennial problems that often arises in prehistory: how was this or that tool used. If it resembles unmistakably a tool used by modern primitives than it is likely that the prehistoric toolmaker used it in the same way. There are a large number of stone and bone tools whose original function eludes us. Semenov, the Soviet author, by studying the traces of work on the tool, usually under magnification, could detect the direction of movement of the work and so infer how it was likely to have been used. The difficulty in the inference is that we do not usually know what the prehistoric person was doing. I fear the results of this kind of study have not really come up to expectation.

My third translation, entirely my own choice and the most important, was composite work drawing upon ten or more different Soviet publications. The waterlogged site at Novgorod in the medieval town had already achieved fame in the Soviet Union because of the birch bark notes, written in Russian, found in the excavations, but from the western point of view it was the skill of the excavator (B.A. Kolchin) in revealing the streets of half logs laid crosswise 27 times from the earlier middle ages with the associated houses that astonished our own scholars. Tree-ring chronology hardly known in the west at that time gave a detailed dating and a fine hoard of dirhems at the bottom completed the picture. *Novgorod the Great* really showed that medieval archaeology could transform our knowledge so limited in the written records of this area, The replacement of the street level seems to have taken place each generation and the log-built houses adjoining had to follow suit. Only the bottom frame of each house survived but it was inferred that some had more than one storey. The change from larger to smaller houses over the period suggested a change from the occupants being mainly merchants to craftsmen in small workshops. The birch bark messages were like telegrams or e-mails although it is rarely that we can identify the sender or recipient. The discovery indicated a much higher level of literacy than expected among the Russians in this area; there were almost certainly foreign trading stations on the other side of the river that divides the town. There was of course no summary like mine of the excavation in Russian which may have indeed been helpful to them.

Artsikhovsky was the person in overall charge but he seems to have been only interested in the birch-bark messages while the man running the excavation was Kolchin with whom I was in correspondence. I wrote in English and he replied in Russian. I usually corresponded with the author (except Mongait!) about obtaining the illustrations since dealing with the Soviet Trade Delegation presented problems as those who have tried it will know. As the 'cold war' was in full swing I was nervous about getting the authors into trouble although all survived. They were usually flattered by a western translation and Rudenko provided an altered text and rewrote the introduction to his work. Although Mongait was commercially successful Novgorod was intellectually the most satisfying and is still in use for teaching in universities.

The last of my translations was also by invitation; earlier Russian translations had aroused interest in the subject so I was invited by Dents to chose a Russian work for this treatment. I chose Sergei Rudenko's account of his excavations at Pazyryk in the Pamir mountains. It was not a technical *tour de force* like Novgorod but being made in the *permafrost* in the mountains preservation was remarkable of objects that rarely survive in normal burials. The burials were in shafts below a mound covering them. There had been some attempt to rob them before so they were not quite virgin deposits.

This is not the place to describe the work but a few of the main points may be useful to the reader. The dead were buried with their horses and riding equipment. The bodies were of course clothed and the surviving skin was in some cases tattooed with elaborate patterns. They had wheeled vehicles, rather primitive trolleys, and a very sophisticated wagon that has a Chinese look. Although the art motifs suggested links to Persia and the Scythian nomads of the steppe the site was sufficiently far east to feel the influence of China. The date was thought to be fifth century BC although radiocarbon may have corrected that.

Although the circumstances of the cold war and the initiative of Sir Allen Lane caused the translations to be made they seem to have had a permanent influence both in British and European archaeology to judge by the continued activity in Novgorod and on use-traces on tools. Russia is no longer a land of mystery known only to a few classicists like Sir Ellis Minns but is now open to the most humdrum of scholars; it is a part of the curriculum in universities. Without blowing one's own trumpet too much I believe the exercise was eminently worthwhile.

8 · Ancient Monuments and the Civil Service

Before turning to the thirty years I spent in the civil service, twenty in London and ten in Cardiff, I will mention where I actually lived during this period after leaving Cambridge in 1954. First I was in bed-and breakfast accommodation in Ebury Street, near Victoria station, a short bus ride from the Ministry of Works at Lambeth Bridge House, now demolished, opposite the gateway of Lambeth Palace. I left there in 1960 with a new car, my first, and went to Hampstead to share a flat with a colleague whose marriage had broken down, but only for a few months as the owner wanted the full house for a married daughter. I moved to Raynes Park to a bungalow and then in 1965 after marriage I went to Claygate, Surrey, having watched the house rise from its foundations. I left there for Cardiff in 1974 on taking charge of the branch there and completed the circle by returning to Cambridge in 1984 on retirement.

Before joining the Ministry of Works I had been steered by John Hurst into doing 'rescue' excavations for the Ministry, at this date John having already been in the Ministry (1953). 'Rescue' excavations were started in the war on archaeological sites threatened by the construction of aerodromes or other military projects. The Chief Inspector of Ancient Monuments, Brian O'Neil, wanted to carry on these after the war on civilian sites. 'Rescue' excavations are the ultimate origin of the elaborate system of trusts that now cover the country performing a similar function. I was caught up with 'rescue' from 1953 to about 1958 so I must deal with them first before turning to my formal entry into the Ministry.

Rescue excavations in 1953 and for some years ahead resembled rather what had happened before the war. In other words there was a supervisor perhaps with an assistant with a labour force consisting of men taken on from the labour exchange. The only expertise was provided by the supervisor. Later on certain rescuers could chose their site and time of year to do the work and even bring volunteers on to the site. I was not among these few and as threats could happen at any time of the year even on scheduled sites as the Act only allowed three months notice. At one of my

Michael Thompson ▪ Cambridge, 2012

sites, Huttons Ambo in Yorkshire, much of the work proceeded in deep snow. It was entirely different from the situation as it is today which will be described shortly.

I tackled nine sites that arose at random and published the results in two cases in national journals and the others in local journals. The Ministry subsidised the cost of publication. I will briefly mention the more significant ones. The only prehistoric site was the remains of a barrow overhanging a gravel pit near the Hardy Monument, Portesham, Dorset. It was very exposed place in wind and rain but in the rare sun commanded a splendid view over the sea. The inner turf mound was strikingly black with white streaks from the sods and with the yellow gravel heaped on top must have looked like Saturn with its ring formed by the freshly dug ditch. Late bronze age urns had been inserted in the mound but no trace of an original burial was found.

Two "moats" at Epperstone and Grantham only yielded modern finds (clay pipes) with no building enclosed. Whether they were for fish, watering stock, duck decoy or even ornamental it is impossible to say. They clearly demonstrated that not all 'moats' marked on the OS sheets held a medieval house. Far more satisfying was the excavation at Seasalter Level, near Whitstable, Kent, where the great storm of 1953 had flooded the marsh on which lay a number of shapeless mounds thought by the Ordnance Survey to be geological in origin but evidently remains of medieval salt extraction. Excavation of a mound produced wood items, lead (presumably from boiling pans) leather shoes. The mounds evidently for huts above tide level must have been in use before the sea wall cut off the tide and with written sources showing the struggles with the sea embankment evidently took place from the early fourteenth century.

A real medieval moat at Anlaby near Hull had little surviving structures but was of interest in that it yielded some painted ware imported from France. The site is described in the Anlaby Chartulary in Pembroke College Cambridge where the writer laments that he had lost it to Haltemprice Priory. The fragment of a Roman barrow in Essex and the Cistercian grange at Ropsley. Lincolnshire sadly not fully explored may be mentioned. The most rewarding undoubtedly was at Huttons Ambo, near Malton, a fortified enclosure overlooking the river Derwent. Here a single aisled hall was found and sherds of 12th century pottery. The occupant of the site was probably Colswain who held it by keeping the gate of the king's castle at York. Unlike the 'Time Team' of today I had no mechanical aids nor an abundant supply of skilled or semiskilled labour but of course usually more time.

No doubt the work had its value but the problem in all 'rescue archaeology' was that it was haphazard not allowing study of a single subject in a scholarly fashion. The ministry was ill-adapted to this type of work and there is no doubt that its replacement by outside trusts today is a big improvement. Furthermore bringing scheduled monuments into the planning system makes it easier to resist development so then reducing the risk of hasty and unforeseen excavation. This has happened long after I had left the Ministry and is not for me to discuss.

Some excellent work was done and published by rescue diggers notably Hope-Taylor at Yeavering in Northumberland on the Saxon palace. After I joined the Ministry in 1954 I was concerned with organising rescue digs and thereby hangs a different story. There were same supervisors who would not or perhaps could not write up the results of their work where information may have been lost. These were the only ones we got to turn out in mid-winter which put us in a difficult position; it was a dilemma that caused me endless worry.

It is time to turn to my formal admission to the Ministry in 1954: I arrived at Lambeth Bridge House at the appointed time where copies of the 1913 and 1931 Acts were thrust into my hands and I was told to go upstairs where the required work would be found for me. Such was my introduction to the Ministry of Works; I may at this point give some account of the organisation and how the Acts were put into force.

We were not an outside quango like the British Museum or English Heritage but within a Ministry. At that time the standard Ministry had three grades the administrators who entered the civil service by examination, were clever and usually able with grades from Principal to Permanent Secretary at the top. Below were three or four grades of executive officers with clerical officers at the bottom of the heap. The ancient monuments department consisted of professional officers of two kinds: architects who looked after the monuments in care and controlled a large industrial staff on the ground.

Michael Thompson ▪ Cambridge, 2012

and ancient monument inspectors who had an advisory function which often became virtually executive.

The triangle of administrator, architect and inspector gave rise to rancour but when there was a benign Permanent Secretary it could work well to which the great volumes of *the History of the King's Works* bear witness. The simple solution of putting monuments in a professional organisation outside government proposed by Lubbock in the 1870's has to a high degree been met by the creation of English Heritage in the 1980's. This is particularly so when as now (2011) the Chief Executive is a professional. The present day organisation is indeed hardly recognisable as the descendant of that which operated in my time and these differences to which we must now turn are fundamental.

During my time three or four hundred industrial staff were employed on maintaining the monuments organised regionally under a superintendent all controlled by the architects. English Heritage as I understand it has no architects and no industrial staff; all work is done by contract. It is the old question of which is preferable contract or direct labour? The former gives flexibility but permanent mundane maintenance may suffer without the latter. The reader must visit the monuments and judge for himself. During my time with the Ministry the industrial staff and custodians were an essential feature of the background so I have had to devote some space to them.

I said that in my early years I was still concerned with rescue excavation in the field but in 1958 I 'moved' to the England section regarded as the real core of ancient monuments protection and preservation, concerned as it was with 'scheduling' and monuments in Ministry care. The Chief Inspector had been impressed by my Pickering Castle guide. The former I will turn to later but the latter could involve excavation so needs attention here.

The Ministry had over three hundred monuments in its care, usually in guardianship with freehold title remaining in the hands of the owner. When these came into care they had normally been neglected for years, even centuries and consequently were overgrown and buried in fallen material. Masonry was dealt with by our architects, craftsmen and labourers but the inspectors were concerned with retrieval and treatment. This could lead to great surprises of which Farnham is in some sense a classic example so will be dealt with here.

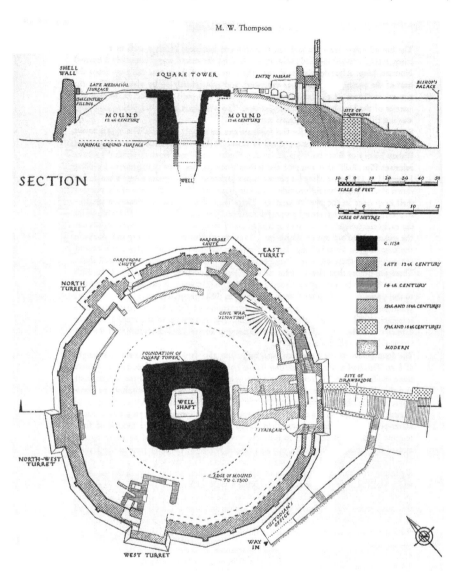

Fig. 2 ▪ *Farnham Castle, Surrey: section through the keep from my excavation 1958 showing well shaft, expanded tower base at top over motte.*

Original tower perhaps demolished on orders of Henry II.

Michael Thompson ▪ Cambridge, 2012

Fig. 3 ▪ *Farnham Castle: the huge tower base exposed in 1958*

The bishops of Winchester (Medieval owners of the castle) had formed flower beds inside the shell keep pressing against the wall which were thought to be pushing it out. A cross trench over the interior revealed a vast expanse of masonry, one of the most astonishing experiences of my life, and from this followed the discovery of the flange, the buried tower with its well shaft and associated motte which was part of the original work. It was perhaps my greatest contribution to knowledge. It led to my interest in castles and indeed to a private excavation by Peter Curnow and myself at Richards Castle, Herefordshire, where a remarkable polygonal keep or tower was found on top of the motte.

Kenilworth castle, Warwickshire, where I did a great deal at the south end and revealed a postern at the north end; as at Farnham I wrote the usual blue guidebook in 1976. Conisborough castle was another case where I recovered a plan of domestic buildings. Abbeys, priories and so on also needed attention. I was involved at Rufford and Bury St Edmunds abbeys. At Archbishop Chichele's college at Higham Ferrers I was able to demonstrate a reduction in plan during construction perhaps due to shortage of funds.

Fig. 4 ▪ *Farnham Castle: Bishop Wayneflete's brick entry tower, built 1470–75 from foundation to roof dated by author from Winchester manorial accounts*

The ultimate objective of the work was to produce the guidebook with dated plan, the history occasionally being done by an outside scholar. A good example was Dover castle written by the late Dr. Allen Brown The guide could be a significant contribution to knowledge as Gilyard Beer's at Fountains Abbey, Yorkshire. Historians who rely entirely on written sources could have difficulty; an invitation to a distinguished scholar on Conisbrough castle was refused on the grounds that written sources were insufficient to allow a guidebook to be undertaken!

Michael Thompson ▪ Cambridge, 2012

Fig. 5 ▪ *Old Bolingbroke Lincolnshire: the 13th century castle emerging from the turf after our excavation, note polygonal shape with towers on angles*

There was a set pattern to the blue guide published by HMSO: history, description, foldng dated plan at end. There were of course photographs for illustrations and card versions in English and foreign languages. The blue guides were hard work for the general public and the English Heritage guides are easier to handle and read than the blue guides but less consciously exploratory.

I enjoyed writing guides but only did three: Pickering, Farnham and Kenilworth castles. Pickering was perhaps the most enjoyable on account of the area and the wealth of documentary evidence in the Pipe Rolls. The others incorporated excavation evidence about which I have already spoken.

I had little control over actual treatment of the ruins which was exercised by architect and Inspector for England. From time to time I went with them touring a region with architect and superintendent in front, the latter driving.

Fig. 6 ▪ *Conisborough Castle, Yorkshire: the hall revealed by my excavation as seen from the top of the circular 12th century keep.*

Both these have disappeared today as have the craftsmen and labourers whose work we went to see. The removal of the title of Inspector from the legislation (by administrators) allowed the post of Chief Inspector to disappear, presumably to be followed by those with the title. I do not think we need feel any nostalgia; Its results for the monuments that matter.

It is time to turn to the other activity of the inspector, scheduling or trying to prevent interference with monuments which were already scheduled. The 1882 Act had a schedule at the end that is a list of monuments that it sought to protect and the 1913 Act allowed the minister to add to this list as much as he thought necessary, hence the verb to schedule, past participle 'scheduled'. As a result the list ran to several thousand by 1954 and was growing longer rapidly.

The term ancient monument was hugely extended after the war. For example a farmer might blow up a wartime pillbox in 1955 but by 1970 pill boxes were schedulable and hands were held up in horror at blowing one up. The identification of industrial monuments added hundreds of potential schedulable monuments. As with listing by the Ministry of Housing there is no date limit on

Fig. 7 ▪ *South Wingfield Manor, Derbyshire: hall and porch from work started in 1439 from my reading of a later account.*

the structure. In passing it might be mentioned that 'listed' meant inhabited or occupied buildings whereas ancient monuments were ruins or earthworks, inhabited buildings being specifically excluded in the Act.

The Board that had advised the Minister had recommended that all barrows, prehistoric burial mounds, should be scheduled, without exception after many had been damaged by ploughing. Many thousands of these mounds exist. The Crichel Down affair had given rise to some anxiety but we pushed ahead. Walking the Downs to mark up the barrows fortunately already shown on the large-scale OS maps was a not disagreeable job only occasionally disturbed by unusually hostile owners or dogs. Days on the Downs followed by dinner at the hotel and tapping at the typewriter on Russian translation until midnight has left many happy memories.

Although I had done work on excavations by train and taxi scheduling needs a car and I drove from 1960 in my own car claiming 'mileage' for official journeys. A colleague who did much of same work (a wartime SOE officer) said that the two essentials for an inspector were a driving licence and a high crutch to step over barbed wire!

As with much legislation enforcement is a problem. The owner only had to give three months notice to put the Ministry on the spot as to what to do. It could lead to rescue excavation but that was a last resort if no compromise were possible. It led to many journeys. If there was damage or destruction then the question of prosecution arose although understandably the Ministry was reluctant to alienate people by using its powers. I attended court two or three times to give evidence. Inflation had rendered the fines imposed trifling and to my knowledge imprisonment was never imposed.

One must remember that the object of all this activity was to preserve ancient monuments not in the Ministry's care which amounted to many thousands of sites always growing in numbers. Only powers conferred by Parliament could be used for restraints that were sometimes resented leading indeed to only permissive powers being granted in 1882. After the war state interference was taken much for granted and although I met a lack of enthusiasm actual resentment was rare.

'Scheduling' took no account of natural weathering so there was a Canute-like element involved especially with regard to masonry. I hope and think it did slow down destruction but ploughing did and does cause concern leading to the agitation that led to the formation of trusts for rescue excavation. Surveillance by the somewhat ethereal county correspondents was not satisfactory and we must hope that the paid 'wardens' of English Heritage fare better.

Fig. 8 ▪ *Kenilworth Castle: Warwickshire: section through dam/causeway with me pointing to evidence from raising probably in early 13th century.*

9 · Marriage

As the emotional crisis receded from my relationship with my Catalan girlfriend following the passage of years I had much milder encounters with other girls. In one or two cases I made proposals of marriage which were declined, no doubt wisely. One that came to fruition started in a decidedly archaeological setting for I met Ann either on the boat or among the monuments in Denmark during a conference of the Prehistoric Society held there in 1964; we were married in October of that year. Denmark that had been such a propitious place for archaeology was propitious for my life.

It was not of course honey all the way; I had been warned against it by a colleague and my mother-in-law said that I only did it to inherit her money! This is classic mother-in-law thinking. My childhood had been dominated by my brother, Patrick, who was two years older than me and I did not wish to marry a dominating woman. I did not; Ann who was sweetness itself was in no sense forceful or dominating so that in spite of bumpy patches we contrived to live together for 46 years. Only at her death in May 2011 after prolonged illness did I appreciate how much she meant to me.

Six years after our marriage Ann gave birth by caesarian operation to a daughter, Elizabeth, upon whom I lean much in old age. At the time it was a great joy to Ann who had seen herself in spinsterhood looking after her mother. For me it was a great joy also and indeed a relief as I had had misgivings about my potency.

Although we met in an archaeological environment she had a limited interest in this and went through various subjects such as bridges, perhaps only recent military history and war cemeteries being permanent. She arranged for us to visit the grave of my uncle (whom I never knew). Roy Welman, killed in Gallipoli in 1915 as an Anzac soldier; the grave had probably never been visited since he was buried there.

Ann's permanent interest was music for she was an instrumentalist playing the harp, violin and viola. The harp makes a beautiful sound but weighs

Fig. 9 ■ *Ann Elizabeth Thompson in c1984*

a hundredweight with sharp foot pedals striking the carrier's ankles and also requires a van or estate car to move it about. In due course it was sold and she continued to play with orchestras on violin and later viola in Cardiff and Cambridge. I often was in the audience when she played with the Cambridge Philharmonic Orchestra especially if it was in Trinity or Kings chapels. I am no musician without an ear for it but liked listening with Ann to concerts or the Proms.

Ann sometimes accompanied me on my constant travels and excavations. She had a van for the harp when we first married but subsequently had my old car for I changed every two and half years while I was working. Having driven for 50 years I lost the car in a skid in 2010 when it hit a lamp post and was a written-off; at 81 it seemed the right time to give up driving.

Our daughter went first to a Roman Catholic school in Cardiff and then on my retirement to a village college in Cambridgeshire. She obtained a diploma in printing at Manchester and now works in that field near where I live in Newton. She is married and with my son-in-law has been a great help to me during my wife's incapacity for in the years before her death she had a deteriorating problem with walking, something akin to Parkinsons disease which happily did not affect her faculties. Since her death my daughter and son-in-law have been unstinting in their help to the author now of course a widower.

10 · Wales

I left the London office of the Ministry, with now changed title of Ministry of Public Building and Works, later the Department of the Environment, and much later on even English Heritage when it left Government altogether, in September 1974. Officially on loan from the Department of Environment to the Welsh Office (after I left formally under the Welsh Assembly and known as *Cadw*). I had the title Head of Ancient Monuments Branch in Wales conferred by the Department of the Environment but probably rescinded by the Welsh Office. There was an Assistant Secretary lurking in the background who was the administrative superior over the professional officer.

The first few years of my time in Wales were among the happiest in the public service; I had an impressive title albeit with limited solid authority; I had a staff of two or three inspectors only too willing to show me the ropes. The organisation was small compared to that in London so that one could readily grasp how it worked. We had 120 or so monuments in care compared with 300 or 400 in England; the industrial staff were correspondingly less under their superintendent, a plumber by trade with the attributes of the profession. One could go home for lunch so there was no question of living the commuter life of London. The Welsh countryside was of intoxicating beauty, especially up through central Wales. Our principal monuments were in north Wales and the office was in Cardiff so travelling north/south through the centre of Wales was frequently necessary. We had a pleasant house and both my wife and daughter liked Wales becoming reluctant to leave it when I retired.

It must be remembered that I went to Wales against a background of rising nationalism which is very relevant to the monuments. This point is best made by comparison with Scotland where the monuments are held in greater esteem than in Wales because largely created by the Scots themselves which makes it easier to identify with, In Wales the main monuments in care of the state are castles like those of Edward 1 constructed to confirm the conquest of the country or by Anglo-Norman barons of decidedly non-Welsh origin. Even the Roman remains are emblems of conquest: forts not villas and a few insignificant towns. Even in later times there are scarcely any great country houses; the society that produced them in England was not there. We admire the work of Burges in Cardiff and at Castell Coch (in state care) but the architect who built them was English and his employer Scottish, the Marquess of Bute.

If it is difficult to identify with the monuments how does nationalism express itself in Wales? The answer is of course in the language which although it is only the first language of 20% of the population has an almost sacred character as the very essence of Welshness. The motorist as soon as he enters Wales finds bilingual signs to remind him of this. The ancient monuments branch or *Cadw*, literally keeping (*heneblon*, old things for monuments hardly suggests heritage!) We had to take account of this and had summaries in Welsh in our guidebooks. That to 'Strata Florida' a Cistercian abbey with special Welsh connections I left without an English translation when I left Wales but I Imagine the demands of sales have caused one to be made since then.

Welsh is a Celtic language of the p-family (like Cornish and Breton) but unlike Irish of the q-family has shed its declensions but both of course have mutations, Its great virtue is its almost phonetic spelling so you can pronounce it when you see it which is not true of Irish. The grammar and vocabulary are very unfamiliar and I fear I never fully mastered them.

Ignoring for the moment the ambivalent attitude of Welsh people to their monuments let us discuss the main monuments in care in the Principality. We may turn to the castles of Edward 1 in north Wales which gave the main revenue and attracted about a million of our two million visitors in a holiday area attracting many tourists from outside.

The Edwardian castles in Wales stand out from others in the British Isles in three respects: first the documents in the National Archives recording their construction are almost complete and have been comprehensively studied by the late Arnold Taylor, Chief Inspector of Ancient Monuments and fully published in *The History of the Koing's Works*, 1. chapter six (293-394), 2, 1027–1040. Taylor also studied archives in Switzerland that throw light on the Savoyard craftsmen who took part in the work, notably James of St Georges, whom he regarded as the architect of the principal castles of the second campaign. Second the castles, albeit empty shells are sufficiently intact to associate the documents with the relevant castle. Thirdly the main four or five castles hardly underwent alteration in the years following their construction. As Taylor wrote guidebooks to most of them there was no need for further research at the time I was there.

The castles of the two campaigns of 1277 and 1283 were different in character: those of 1277 being fairly heterogeneous but those of 1283 share much more in common. It is to the latter that we will confine attention, particularly the four attributed by Taylor to James of St Georges: Harlech, Carnarvon, Conway and Beaumaris. The first three were started in 1283 and Beaumaris in 1295. Two of these. Harlech and Beaumaris were geometric square shapes with double 'concentric' curtain walls but on the other hand at Carnarvon and Conway the form of the castle was dictated by the rock on which it stands. Conway unlike the other three lacked a massive gatehouse. The point I am driving at is that the castle was designed first and that the domestic buildings fitted in as best as possible. Even at Carnarvon and Conway the division into two was suggested by the narrow rock formation turned to advantage. A former Chief Inspector. Brian O'Neill defined a castle as a 'fortified house' but these examples, as well as many others suggest a better definition would be 'a fortification with a dwelling in it' It is good that Patrick Faulkner set us all off on analysing the domestic accommodation in castles but it is surely unbalanced to believe that a castle's design was only worked out by how it was to be lived in.

In south Wales there are two or three remarkable castles in care: Caerphilly just north of Cardiff and Raglan in Monmouthshire. The former with a quadrilateral design with towers at the corners and in front a fortified barrier or dam to hold back streams thus creating two lakes on either side of the castle. It recalls Leeds castle in Kent with its waterworks but the restorations by the Marquess of Bute have altered its appearance. It was non-royal but reminds one of Beaumaris which is 25 years later; It seems to have been known to the builders of Edward I's castles. Raglan is a splendid fifteenth century structure with a hexagonal keep with provision for firearms which suffered in the civil war and from slighting after-wards.

In this land of castles one that cannot be omitted which made a deep impression on me was Castell Coch (the red castle) a few miles north of

Cardiff. There had been a small thirteenth century castle here the ruins of which were entirely restored by William Burges for the Marquess of Bute, who recorded its condition before work began and as proposed (slightly altered in the real thing). Burges was familiar with the work of Viollet-le-Duc in France so it is very realistic externally while inside he let his imagination run free on furniture and decoration. There was a vineyard to go with the castle that produced its own brand of wine, the Marquess of Bute who had become a Catholic convert took a great interest in the work.

The monastic ruins in Wales are less impressive than in England for I was used to the great Cistercian abbeys in Yorkshire. The exception is Tintern by the river Wye on the border with England again a large Cistercian abbey leaving a fine ruin. The literary connections are slender as Wordsworth only uses the name in the title of his poem. Unfortunately the tourist does not reach it by boat from the river as he did in the early nineteenth century, as described by Colt Hoare.

Happily there was only one major dispute about preservation while I was in Wales which was the Conway bridge crossing. The castle had at its eastern end a separate, entry from the estuary which had to be crossed by boat. Thomas Telford constructed a suspension bridge over the river in front of the castle. This was followed later in the nineteenth century by a railway bridge close by and in the twentieth century by the road bridge then carrying the main road from the west.

The proposal was to construct a new motorway-style bridge, a fourth bridge adjoining the castle. This was strongly opposed on the grounds that it would spoil the impressive view of the castle because of its motorway scale. The Secretary of State for Wales was anxious to proceed speedily to relieve the summer congestion but the Transport Minister was opposed to it on amenity grounds. I was in a difficult position since there was responsibility to both Ministers. The opposition to the proposal was led by the retired Chief Inspector of Ancient Monuments, Arnold Taylor, whom I supported and even contemplated resignation in the heat of the moment. Happily a splendid solution was found for the road was put in a tube resting on the river bed, a recently developed method, and that is how the river is crossed today, which the reader may indeed have driven through. It is slightly downstream from the castle which is hardly affected.

By 1984 I had been in Wales nine years on loan and then formally and physically in the Welsh Office. In England English Heritage was created in 1984 but in Wales Cadw, was created slightly later after I had left; it has since come under the Welsh Assembly. I had became a little ill at ease in the new environment and so was pleased to take early retirement. My wife had been evacuated to Cambridge during the war so we both had links with the city while I wanted to use the University Library so we sold the house in Cardiff and moved to a village a little to the south-west of the city.

II ▪ Medieval Archaeology

I have served as president of two societies: the Cambridge Antiquarian Society and the Society for Medieval Archaeology. For the former I wrote a brief history on the occasion of its 150th anniversary in 1990, so it seems appropriate that I should give some account of the much younger society that has indeed only just celebrated its 50th anniversary. To some extent it came into being as a result of the activities of the body that employed me.

When the antiquity of man was revealed to the Victorians the next problem, how could the people of such a vast period of time who left no written records be studied? Starting in Denmark various methods of doing this were worked out and as late as 1935 a society was formed by dropping its former regional title to become the *Prehistoric Society* devoted to the study of those distant periods. Could the techniques of prehistory be valid when applied to later literate periods? The older antiquarian societies who tended to specialise in art forms, art history, at first said no. However we all know of Grahame Clark and Piggott prehistorians scraping the traces of the ship at Sutton Hoo, Suffolk, in 1939 and they were prehistorians, Willy-nilly prehistoric methods came to medieval sites. It only needed this application to be recognised in the form of a society for this to take place. The plethora of medieval 'rescue' excavations and the interest in deserted Villages associated with Maurice Beresford and the excavations at Wharram Percy, Yorkshire, by Golson and later John Hurst, demonstrated the need.

I was not myself party to the foundation of the Society and had indeed thought the flurries of excitement would give birth to a general journal like O.S. Crawford's *Antiquity* in the 1920·s. Three people were the mid-wives for the birth of the new society, two museum men and a field worker; Donald Harden, Director of the London Museum keen on and experienced in editing at Oxford who gave the project respectability (Sir) David Wilson and John Hurst of the Ministry of Works. The last two were young at the time. Deserted villages gave common ground with historians, like Professor Carus Wilson elected to the presidency in the early years.

I only came in at a later stage as Review Editor dealing also with notes. I was able to use this position to briefly describe my work on guardianship monuments, notably at Kenilworth, Conisbrough and Bolingbroke castles, and the remarkable shrinking of the plan at Archbishop Chichele's college at Higham Ferrers. It was a most interesting and valuable experience and certainly saved from oblivion work on Ministry monuments. I had trouble with reviewers producing their reviews, a very old problem, and so fell out with other officers of the Society.

Over 50 volumes of *Medieval Archaeology*, our journal, have been published and many monographs so there has been a very solid contribution to knowledge in spite of the journal having difficulty in locating a real niche. It is very difficult to reconcile two sides who have such different methods of working and who tend to be disdainful of each other. This is not the place to discuss these matters at length which we may hope will resolve themselves.

Very important medieval research has been published not only by the society but in the older journals which cannot be described in what purports to be an autobiography although I will be vain enough to mention my own contributions. In my own work I much value the summary of the Novgorod excavations (no such work exists in Russian) still used in teaching and in some ways giving an example of how medieval archaeology should be done. The excavation in the keep at Farnham castle gave on an impressive scale the relations between motte and keep resolving a lot of controversy at the time leading to my own books on castles. Appendices 1 and 3 give my own contributions to the subject of medieval archaeology and where they were published.

Similar journals devoted to the archaeology of specific periods have followed the examples such as *Britannia* and the journal of the Society for Post-Medieval Archaeology ('post-medieval' is 'early modern' for historians), which suggests it set a course to be followed by other disciplines. This would indicate that the venture had been a success.

There are difficulties indeed in the concept of 'medieval archaeology' which may embrace art history or history or numismatics and so on. For example the splendid first two volumes of *The History of the King's Works* treat royal architecture entirely from written sources contemporary with the buildings reversing the role of material remains illustrating written sources. The material remains can be regarded as artistic creations, the usual museum attitude, which takes us into the field of art history. The borders of medieval archaeology have to be elastic to include situations of this kind. I started life as an historian and in medieval archaeology I have attached great weight to the written sources while still accounting myself an archaeologist. Broadly speaking the areas in which written sources are weak or deficient or unreliable medieval archaeology takes a leading role, where was our knowledge of the seventh century before the discovery of the Sutton Hoo boat burial with Bede alone to guide us?

12 ▪ Books and Travel

When I retired in the spring of 1984 I was still in my mid-fifties, physically active but with no clear idea of what I intended to do except that I would return to Cambridge with which both my wife (who had been evacuated there) and myself had close connections. I wanted to use the University library and to be within easy striking distance of London for society meetings; so although after nine years in Cardiff my wife and daughter did not want leave I felt certain they would rapidly re-adapt to England which they did. I was worried about money since the pension only started at 60 so I had an interview for a Belfast chair, applied for a job with the Church Commissioners and took American parties around Welsh castles. However my father died in 1985 leaving some money (badly reduced by collapse of the *rand*), my wife's shares paid an excellent dividend, the maturing insurance mortgage giving a healthy sum; all combined to put me in a comfortable position allowing me to embark on the writing and travel to which the chapter heading refers.

Before turning to these a word about my reasons for my choosing to live six miles outside the town of Cambridge. Our first house was at Hardwick which we intended as a temporary stop until we found a permanent place which we did in Newton in December 1986. A bungalow (a wise choice as it turned out) with a large garden in a village with an active life of its own and a shop with a post office (sadly now closed) and a public house close at hand met our requirements very well. I did not want to be in the town, cheek by jowl with the university looking at it but really not of it, while undergraduates made one depressingly conscious of one's age. As I no longer drive, the car being a write-off after a skid, the country has lost some of its attraction but not to the extent of changing my mind. The time for family travels had ended when my daughter became independent so my journeys started in 1991, normally alone in a party, occasionally with my wife but her increasing disability made it difficult for her. They always had an archaeological or architectural slant preceded by some study beforehand, and were well equipped with maps and a guidebook. It was a kind of modified tourism intended to give a general impression, never returning to the same place a second time. The 39 journeys are listed in Appendix 2 and I will merely comment on some of them here.

1991 May, to Greece where I had not been before, Mycenae and the Schlieman treasures in Athens particularly impressed me. In November a trip up the Nile which had been delayed by the first Iraq war.

1992 In April to Crete and Knossos. Reconstruction at the latter odd but perhaps only way to do it. In December Jordan and Syria, impressed by Krak des Chevaliers and much else.

1993 In December Uzbekistan, Samarkand. Shocked by old Soviet hotels.

1994 In May Pompei and Naples area. First *Andante* Journey. In September Venice and surrounding villas with Oxford party.

1995 In March/April China. Shocked by medieval date of masonry of Great Wall I would like to make section through wall to find earlier earthen wall. Impressed by terracotta army. In June to Gallipoli to see uncle's grave. Spent week in area. In September Santiago de Compostella as a sort of pilgrimage from Oxford,return Santander ferry.

1996 August/September Moscow by boat to St Petersburg Memorable trip with wife. Stopped at block-work museum on way.

1997 April Moorish Spain with Oxford. October Apulia, Castel del Monte slept in a *trullo.*

1998 January Hamburg by boat. April Jerusalem with Martin Biddle. October Sicily Splendid Roman mosaics

1999 Tunisia with Andante. Contrast between north and south. June/July St Petersberg Scythian, gold at the Hermitage. Novgorod. September with Royal Archaeological Institute to Burgundy. October Central Italy for monasteries and Rome

2000 March/April North Portugal for monasteries and Port wine at Oporto. September Lebanon

2001 April Libya September Catalunya-much nostalgia. Went into Gaudi building in *Ramblas*. Tarragona

Michael Thompson ▪ Cambridge, 2012

2002 May Peru First encounter with Inca area. October Bulgaria

2003 February/March Guatemala impressed and surprised by Mayan hieroglyphics. April Malta with RAI. Temples. November Mexico Late Maya

2004 March Avignon Palace and Pont du Gard. May Crimea with Ann. Alma battlefield, Sevastopol, Yalta. September/October Persia, Iran Isfahan.

2005 January/February Rajasthan Taj Mahal Curzon restorations October/November Cambodia Angkor Wat-its scale impressive.

2006 May Turkey Central. Çatal Höyük. September Turkey, Eastern bathed in Lake Van.

2007 April Turkey Western, September Rhineland Charlemagne, trip on Rhine

Brief journeys like this must necessarily be superficial for experience on monuments suggests even on small monuments at least three or four visits needed to understand what you see. Nevertheless one's mind is no longer a blank when you hear the name. It certainly broadens the mind although would have been better done in youth. I hardly mention Classical monuments although these were most common, particularly theatres, yet I was left with an abiding consciousness of the extent and depth of Classical culture in the Mediterranean world.

Running side by side with my travelling I wrote several books. If we exclude the Russian translations already described in chapter 7 then there were three books written in Wales before retirement. A complete list of my books will be found in Appendix 1, and to make the bibliography a little nearer complete I have added a select list of articles and guidebooks mostly written well before retirement in Appendix 3.

1977 The first book I wrote was *General Pitt-Rivers, evolution and archaeology in the nineteenth century*. My interest in the subject had arisen when the General's notebooks as Inspector of Ancient Monuments came to light followed later by papers of his grandson, George Pitt-Rivers, which were however of limited value, my own interest in evolution and archaeology culminated, one might say consummated, in my account of John Lubbock in 2009.

1981 *Ruins, their preservation and display*. Published by British Museum Publications gave an account of preservation as practised by the Department of Environment.

1983 *The journeys of Sir Richard Colt Hoare through Wales and England*, 1793-1810. There are two sets of his diaries in the City Library in Cardiff that he kept on the road in his travels. One set is a fair copy (damaged) and the other the original I assume of what he wrote on the way which I used for a very short summary of six volumes, omitting the one dealing with Ireland. He was interested in the picturesque and made many drawings prints of which are held in the National Library of Wales. I fear the subject and the author make little appeal to Welshmen.

1987 Now at Cambridge and the next book was published by the University Press. Since the excavations at Farnham castle this subject has been a major interest, *The Decline of the Castle*. The recent re-issue as a paper-back and the PLR figures suggest that it was useful piece of work, historians have been interested in the Civil War 'slighting'.

1990 *The Cambridge Antiquarian Society, 1840-1990*. This was to celebrate. the 150th anniversary; a copy is now given to each new member of the Society. I had full access to the Society's bulky records.

1991 *The Rise of the Castle* also published by CUP with recent paperback edition. This is rather an overworked subject and not selling as well as the *Decline*. The reversal of the chronological order is accidental without special significance.

1995 *The Medieval Hall*. An absorbing subject but I would write it very differently today.

1998 *Medieval bishops' houses in England and Wales*. Broke new ground and I remain pleased with it.

2001 *Cloister, abbot and precinct in medieval monasteries*. Based very much on ruins in state care using plans in blue guides. I enjoyed writing it hope it is useful even if basic but fairly original.

2006 *Ruins reused: changing attitudes to ruins since the late eighteenth century*. Thoughts prompted by the Colt Hoare travels and brought me back to nineteenth century and evolution.

2009 *Darwin's pupil: the place of Sir John Lubbock, Lord Avebury (1834–1913) in late Victorian and Edwardian England*. The publication of Darwin's letters and the availability of Emma Darwin's diary has thrown much light on the connections between Lubbock and Darwin; although all Lubbock's activities are touched on in this book it was intended as a fitting end to my writing in retirement.

Appendix 3 lists selectively my more important articles and guidebooks mostly from before my retirement and so not strictly belonging to this chapter. My interests over fifty years can be followed: prehistory in Azilian harpoons, various rescue excavations of which Huttons Ambo and Seasalter are the most interesting. The first green guidebook to Pickering castle took me into medieval manuscripts which it can be seen now play a bigger part, of which South Wingfield was the most interesting. Pitt-Rivers tended to bring me back to evolution and the history of archaeology, almost back to prehistory. My only venture into literary archaeology was with *Sir Gawain*; among other things I was able to correct the misreading 'bantels' (a nonsense) to 'bautels' (bowtels) here using a contemporary word for 'machicolations' only adopted from French in English in the eighteenth century. There are many other interesting items that I could refer to but I will not tax the reader's attention with a description of every article in the list.

I have spent much time describing my travels and publications but what else did I do in 27 years of retirement enjoyed so far. This third of my life has been perhaps the most contented, not short of money, not pursuing the baubles of jobs, living in a large bungalow with a comfortable study, a large garden to sit in during the summer, friends and relatives sadly dropping out (my brother Patrick died in 1996, his widow in 2008, leaving four children now middle-aged}, culminating in the death of my wife in May 2011. The idyll must be concluded alone, happily with my daughter and son-in-law to support me. The loss of my car in a winter skid and not replaced has made me rely on taxis.

I have kept up professional activities as long as possible with the various societies and made frequent visits to London for lectures with various bodies usually proceeded by the exhibitions which are constant source of interest in London. I have dining rights at the College which I occasionally use. Fortunately my health holds and I was recently able to lecture in the British Museum.

13 · Reflections

As a boy of 17 I remember hearing through the bedroom wall my grandfather shortly before his death say to his wife 'Je ne regrette rien'. I recollect the shock I felt that an old man should regret nothing in his long life and frankly thought that it was an improbable exaggeration. Now older slightly than he was when he spoke to my grandmother in 1946 I see the matter in a different light, although I would not repeat his claim for myself.

I should say at once that I in no way look down on his life: earning a comfortable living and pension, seven children, retirement to a thatched cottage with a large garden, not unhealthy, rock-solid marriage........ what more could a man want ? No doubt he did at this or that time regret this or that decision but it is the cumulative effect of all the decisions, right or wrong, that landed him up in the position he was in when he spoke and he was thinking in terms of a life-time with an impending conclusion. To that extent I would go along with him. In fact the area of unpredictability is so great that you can only lake judgements retrospectively; chance is an almost overriding factor from the moment of conception.

Chance has certainly been a major factor in my life. Suppose I had plumped for the colonial service as a career in 1950 where would I have ended up? If Clarke had not wanted to know about upper palaeolithic antler work and not met Luis Pericot where would I have been ? So it goes on; the guesses are endless. I doubt whether it is very profitable to pursue that line.

One's personality once laid down in childhood, mainly genetically but with an environmental factor, is the permanent element in the rest of one's life. It is difficult to judge one's own personality but there are certain shortcomings like limited self-confidence, solitariness, proneness to exaggerated alarm, bad temper and so on that are conspicuous. Given the limitations of personality did I achieve a life that took account of these shortcomings and went as far as I could within those limits imposed by them?

I did not think so at the time for there seemed to be numerous disappointments in jobs sought after or abortive proposals of marriage. Looking back after 40 or 50 years one can see that in nearly every case there was unconscious intervention, not supernaturally but psychologically by something like Freud's *Superego* that decided it was a wrong course of action, not compatible with personality and denied it success. The girl friend in Barcelona, still a painful memory, is another example, or the interview for the Belfast chair, an absurd mistake but not painful. I was unsuited to teaching at a University and there was no comparison with the job from which I had just retired. I had had an excellent employer retiring on a generous pension having left an absorbing job that included wide travelling without the rather insular ethos of a university. Even my youthful desire to enter the British Museum for a job held over once or twice (something of a scandal) I can regard with equanimity, and I had the satisfaction of turning down the offer of a museum curatorship in my forties. Experience has taught me that I have a distaste for rows of small finds in glass cases. The fact is the job I had in ancient monuments was among the best of archaeological ways of earning a living, certainly for me with my personality.

I am going some of the way with my grandfather but I do not, like *Candide*, see myself in the best possible of all worlds with its constant disillusionments; the world is neutral and indifferent to the people in it. It is clear that 'chance" plays a huge part in events. I had a reasonably happy marriage but meeting my prospective wife was entirely by chance. Things might have been very different. Even my employment in the Ministry of Works might not have happened if my valued friend from Cambridge days, the late John Hurst, had not pushed the matter with the Chief Inspector, the late Brian O' Neil. So it goes on, chance creates the opportunity but a decision has to be made to ignore it or seize it. Of course one may seize a false opportunity which is not really to your advantage and your 'superego' has to extricate you.

Between the 1930's and today great technological and social changes have taken and are taking place; some like flying, central heating, or television have played a major or part in my life, even if much gadgetry like mobile phones or computers have passed me by. Some changes like fashions in clothing sweep one along even if one falls a little behind. Major social changes, particularly the position of women and the common replacement of marriage by simple co-habitation have not directly affected me, although one is bound to respond to social changes in one's outlook and behaviour.

In archaeology I have long since been out of the main stream, standing on the bank as it were. Prehistory has changed out of all recognition because of the exact dating now possible although the earlier upheavals of the 1960's and 1970's have now been assimilated. The whole background of 1950 when I entered the subject has been transformed and like the 'world market' in economics 'world archaeology' has become the real dimension of the subject. Classical and medieval archaeology have not experienced change on this scale although progress from new discoveries is being made all the time. In my own subject of castles it is rather ideas more than discoveries that tend to proliferate almost out of control. As an onlooker who writes about historical archaeology I find myself in a very pleasant position not involved in the disputes to which other participants in the subject are particularly prone.

Of friends it is perhaps invidious to quote names, and few I fear are still alive. I will confine myself to Peter Curnow at whose home at Hopton Castle near the Welsh border in Shropshire I have recently been a guest. He is a friend and colleague from the 1950's whose hospitality I have often enjoyed. Of my teachers of an earlier generation the late Sir Grahame Clark must occupy a special place, the late Arnold Taylor, Chief Inspector of Ancient Monuments taught me much as did the late Sir Howard Colvin with whom I enjoyed tea at his home and college at Oxford. I will happily conclude this essay with memories of these three.

Appendix 1 ▪ Translations and Books by Author

1961   A. L. Mongait, *Archaeology in the USSR*, translated, and adapted by M.W.T.

1964   S. A. Semenov, *Prehistoric Technology*, translated by M.W.T.

1967   *Novgorod the Great, Excavations at the Medieval City, 1951-62 directed by A. V. Artsikhovsky and B.A. Kolcbin*, compiled by M.W.T.

1970   S. Rudenko, *Frozen Tombs of Siberia, the Pazyryk burials of Iron-Age horsemen*, translated, and edited by M.W.T.

1977   *General Pitt-Rivers, evolution and archaeology in the nineteenth century*

1981   *Ruins, their preservation and display*

1983   *The journeys of Sir Richard Colt Hoare through England and Wales, 1793–1810*, diaries shortened and edited by M.W.T.

1987   *Decline of the castle*

1990   *The Cambridge Antiquarian Society,1840-1990*

1991   *The Rise of the castle.*

1995   *The medieval hall, the basis of secular domestic life 600-1600 AD*

1998   *Medieval bishops' houses in England and Wales*

2001   *Cloister, abbot and precinct in medieval monasteries*

2006   *Ruins reused, changing attitudes to ruins since the late eighteenth century*

2009   *Darwin's pupil: the place of Sir John Lubbock, Lord Avebury (1834–1913) in late Victorian and Edwardian England*

2012   *Reading, writing and archaeology: an autobiographical essay.*

Michael Thompson ▪ Cambridge, 2012

Appendix 2 ▪ Travels 1991-2007 by Author

1991   May 6-13 Greece

       November 7-17 Egypt (University of Warwick)

1992   April 9-16 Crete

       December 14-21 Jordan and Syria (Jules Verne)

1993   October 5-14 Uzbekistan (Jules Verne)

1994   May 2-9 Pompeii etc (Andante)

       September 7-14 Venice (Oxford University)

1995   March 28-April 7 China (Jules Verne)

       June 4-11 Gallipoli

       September 6-20 Santiago de Compostella (Oxford)

1996   August 31-September 11 Russia (Jules Verne)

1997   April 5-17 Muslim Spain (Oxford)

       October 4-11 Apulia (Andante)

1998   January 9-11 Hamburg

       April 17-25 Jerusalem (Biddle)

       October 5-15 Sicily (Andante)

1999   April 22-29 Tunisia (Andante)

       June 25-July 3 St Petersburg (Petteman-Millenium Tours)

       September 12-19 Burgundy (RAI)

       October 21-28 Central Italy (Andante)

2000   March 24-April North Portugal (Ace)

       September 20-28 Lebanon (Andante>

2001   April 10-21 Libya (Andante)

          September 24- 6 October Catalunya (Ace)

2002   May 13-31 Peru (Andante)

          October 11-25 Bulgaria (Ace)

2003   February 15-March 3 Guatemala (Andante)

          April 9-11 Malta (RAI)

          November 3-18 Mexico (Andante)

2004   March17-22 Avignon (?Travel)

          May 2-10 Crimea (War Research)

          September 28-October 10 Persia (The Traveller)

2005   January 18-February 1 Rajasthan (The Traveller)

          October 20-November 11 Cambodia, Laos (Distant Horizons)

2006   May Turkey, Central (Andante)

          September Turkey, Eastern

2007   April Turkey, Western.

          September Rhineland

Appendix 3 ▪ Select List of Articles and Guidebooks by Author

1954 'Azilian harpoons', *Proceedings of Prehistoric Society*, 20,193–211

1955 'Trial excavations at Ropsley grange, near Grantham, Lincolnshire' *Journal of Lincs. Arcbit. and Arcbaeol. Society*. 6, pt. 1. 17–23

1956 'The excavation of the west bailey of a ring motte at Long Buckby Northants.', *Journ. of the Northants. Nat. Hist. Soc. and F. C.,* 33, 55–66

'A group of mounds on Seasalter Level, near Whitstable, and the medieval imbanking against the sea', *Archaeologia Cantiana*, 70, 44–67

'Excavation of a medieval moat at Moat Hill, Anlaby, near Hull', *Yorks. Archaeol. Journ.*, 39, pt.l, 67–85

'Excavation of two moated sites at Cherry Holt. near Grantham, and at Epperstone. near Nottingham'. *Journal of Lincs, Archit, and Archaeol*. Soc 6, pt.2, 72–82

1958 *Pickering Castle, Yorkshire* MoW green guide

1959 'Excavation of the medieval fortified hall of Hutton Colxwain at Huttons Ambo, near Malton', *Archaeological Journal*,116, 69–91

'Excavation of a barrow near the Hardy monument, Blackdown, Portesham. Dorset', *Proceedings of the Prehistoric Society*, 23, 124–36

Conisborough Castle, Yorkshire, HMSO pamphlet guide

1960 'The date of "Fox's Tower", Farnham castle. Surrey', *Surrey Archeol. Collections*, 57, 85–92

Recent excavations in the keep of Farnham castle, Surrey', *Medieval Archaeology*', 4, 81–94

'The first inspector of ancient monuments in the field', *Journal of the British Archaeological Association*, 3rd series, 23, 103–24

Stone age paintings from Castellon. n.d. from an exhibition of reproductions by Porcar shown in the St George's Gallery

1961 *Farnham castle, Surrey*, HMSO blue guide

'Motte substructures', Medieval Archaeology. 5, 305–6

1965 'Marxism and culture', *Antiquity*, 39,108–114

'Two levels of the mere at Kenilworth castle', *Medieval Archaeology* 9,156–161

1966 'The origins of Bolingbroke castle, Lincolnshire', *Medieval Archaeology* 10, 152–158

1967 'Excavations in Farnham castle keep, Surrey, England', *Chateau Gaillard 2,* 100–105

'A contraction in plan at Archbishop Chichele's College, Higham Ferrers, Northants.' *Medieval Archaeology*, 11, 255–57

1968 'A single-aisled hall at Conisbrough castle,Yorkshire', *Medieval Archaeology*, 12, 153

Michael Thompson ▪ Cambridge, 2012

1969   with Peter Curnow, 'Excavations at Richard's Castle, Herefordshire 1962–64' *Journal of the British Archaeological Association*, 3rd ser., 32, 105–27

'Further work at Conisbrough castle, Yorkshire', Medieval Archaeology 13,215-6

'Further work at Bolingbroke Castle, Lincolnshire', *Medieval Archaeology*, 13, 216–20

Conisbrough castle, Yorkshire, DoE pamphlet

1974   *Tattershall castle, Lincolnshire*, National Trust guidebook

1976   'The construction of the manor at South Wingfield in G. Sieveking, I. Longworth and K. Wilson (ed.), *Problems in economic and social archaeology*, London, 417–38

1977   *Kenilworth castle, Warwickshire*, HMSO blue guidebook

1981   'The significance of the buildings of Ralph Lord Cromwell' in A. Detsicas (ed.), *Essays in memory of Stuart Rigold*,155–62

1986   'Associated monasteries and castles in the middle ages: a tentative list'. *Archaeological Journal*. 143, 305–21.

1987   'The abandonment of castles in Wales and the Marches', in J. Kenyon and R. Avent(ed.), *Castles in Wales and the Marches*, 205–17

1969   'The Green Knight's castle' in C, Harper-Bill, C. Holdsworth and J. Nelson (ed.), *Studies in Medieval History presented to R. Allen Brown*.

1991   'The architectural context of Gainsborough Old Hall', *Society of Lincolnshire history and archaeology*, Occasional Papers, 8, 13–20

1992   'Keep or country house? Thin-walled Norman proto-keeps', *Fortress*, 12 13–22

'A suggested dual origin for keeps', *Fortress*,15, 3–15

1993   'Medieval technology in 1492', *Medieval History*, 64–70.

1994   with John Kenyon 'The origin of the word 'keep'. *Medieval Archaeology*, 38, 175–6

'The military interpretation of castles', *Archaeological Journal*, 151 439–445

1997   'Castles' in J. Brewer and J. Gibson (ed.), *A companion to the Gawain poet*, 119–130

1999   with C. Renfrew, 'The catalogues of the Pitt-Rivers Museum, Farnham Dorset, *Antiquity*, 73, 377–93

2004   'The early topography of Lincoln castle in P. Lindley (ed.) in *The early history of Lincoln castle*, Occasional paper, 12, of the Society for Lincolnshire history and archaeology, 23–29

2012   (forthcoming) 'Progress and evolution and changes to the practice of collecting in the mid-nineteenth century' in Jonathan King et al. (ed.) *Turqoise in the Americas; science and conservation, culture and collection.*

9 781780 353838

An environmentally friendly book printed and bound in England by www.printondemand-worldwide.com

This book is made entirely of sustainable materials; FSC paper for the cover and PEFC paper for the text pages.

Reprint of # - C0 - 210/148/7 - PB - Lamination Gloss - Printed on 10-Jan-18 07:26